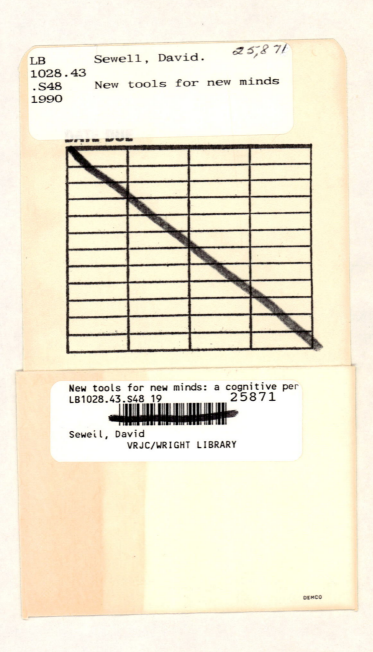

New Tools
for New Minds

New Tools for New Minds

A Cognitive Perspective on the Use of Computers with Young Children

David F. Sewell

St. Martin's Press
New York

First published in the United States of America in 1990

Printed in Great Britain

ISBN 0-312-05575-7

Library of Congress Cataloging-in-Publication Data

Sewell, David.
    New tools for new minds: a cognitive perspective on the use of
computers with young children / David F. Sewell.
        p.   cm.
    Includes bibliographical references (p.   ) and index.
    ISBN 0-312-05575-7
    1. Education—Data processing.   2. Computer-assisted instruction.
3. Cognitive learning.   I. Title.
LB1028.43.$48   1990
371.3'34—dc20   90-44000
                                                                      CIP

To my wife and children
for reminding me of
the important things in life

Contents

Preface

Orientation

As the title of this book implies, its purpose is to utilize a perspective derived from cognitive psychology to consider some of the potential uses of computers with young children. Numerous texts on the educational uses of computers have appeared, but, by and large, these have paid relatively little attention to issues which address the potential cognitive consequences of computer use. If this book has any major objective, it is to draw attention to the close links which exist between educational software, classroom uses of computers and cognitive development. In so doing, the issues addressed draw on themes from a number of subject areas - psychology, education and artificial intelligence being predominant.

However, the purpose is not to go into detail about each of these areas separately – experts in each of these disciplines will readily recognize where specific examples have been simplified, and other areas overlooked. This is a deliberate strategy. Like most areas of investigation, educational computing has been guilty of jargon generation and, at times, of over-complication. I have attempted to steer clear of too much use of jargon, and have made use of such examples as seem relevant to the intended objectives, i.e., to illustrate the potential relationships which exist between the disparate areas feeding into the educational uses of computers. As such, use is made of examples which seem to illustrate particular points, and which are of most relevance to the educational use of computers with young children. By using such examples, my hope is that they will strike a chord with the reader who will perceive their potential relevance to their own situation.

Themes

The dominant theme throughout this book is that computers are a means to an end, and that end is one of cognitive growth. There are two additional aspects to this: computers as used to enable the expression of skills which already exist, and the use of computers to encourage the development of new cognitive skills. Computers are thus seen as cognitive tools, and like any tools, they can be used to make easier the expression of existing skills or to help the user acquire new skills. In order to maintain this emphasis on computers as 'tools of the intellect', their use has to be placed within a framework which emphasizes cognition, learning and information processing, i.e., the perspective adopted within cognitive psychology.

A second major theme concerns the use of Logo, possibly the most significant aspect of educational computing in the 1980s. Logo is important for many reasons, not least because it has a claimed psychological rationale and because many claims have been made for its potential to enhance cognitive functioning. For these reasons alone, Logo is of major importance in any consideration of the relationships between computer use and cognition. However, Logo is significant for other reasons. In many senses the issues raised by the use of Logo act as an exemplar for many educational computing applications. In particular, they address issues of educational philosophy and the extent to which learners can take control of their own educational destinies as opposed to having their destinies decided for them by factors outside their control. The use of Logo thus runs as a second major theme within this book.

Influences

In identifying the major themes to be discussed, I would like to acknowledge three main influences. Inevitably, the first is that of Seymour Papert, Logo and Papert's influential book *Mind-storms*. Papert, Logo and *Mindstorms* have each influenced educational computing in the last decade, and no consideration of the role of computers in education can afford to overlook them. Their impact has been to focus attention on the nature of the claims made for the use of Logo; the role of computers in education, and, on a broader perspective, the extent to which differing philosophies of education interact with the classroom uses of computers.

The second major influence is, paradoxically, scarcely referred to in the educational computing literature. In 1976, David Olson addressed the question of the relationships between technology and cognition, using the example of the development of a writing system. The essence of his argument was that human cognition is dependent on the nature of the technology via which we express our cognitive potential. Olson's thesis is of direct relevance to the nature of the relationships between cognition, software design and computer use, a theme which runs through the material presented here.

The third main influence links directly to the role of computers as a means to enhance cognition. In this context, John Seely Brown's concept of 'empowering environments' is particularly relevant. Such environments enable users to accomplish things that could not otherwise be achieved. The theme in this present book, and in Brown's writing, is that the freeing of cognitive resources is an appropriate use of computers.

Organization

The book is organized loosely into two main sections. Chapters 1–5 provide a theoretically orientated background, and Chapters 6–10 seek to build on this by discussing specific applications, within a broadly cognitive framework. Chapter 1 gives rationales for the use of computers in education, with specific emphasis on their use to promote more effective teaching and learning. In Chapter 2 the use of computers as tools to help foster cognitive expression is discussed. Olson's ideas are used as a basis to explore the role of computers as tools of the intellect. Chapter 3 illustrates differing styles of educational software, their advantages and disadvantages, and shifts in the locus of control from program to user control. Chapter 4 discusses the relationship between software styles and theories of learning; behaviourist and cognitive perspectives on learning, and their implications for the design of computer-mediated materials. In Chapter 5, factors which add to the motivational qualities of software, and their relationship to psychological models of motivation are explored, together with the use of challenge, fantasy and curiosity within software and the enhancement of efficacy and self-esteem.

The second main section of the book begins at Chapter 6 which discusses the use of Logo as exemplifying the links between theory and practice, the nature of the claims made for the use of Logo, the significance of 'bugs', and problems of evaluating and assessing Logo experiences. In Chapter 7 the use of technology to release 'trapped intelligence' in communication-impaired children, the significance of communication and interaction and the role of computers as an 'enabling technology' are discussed. Chapter 8 explores writing as an enabling technology and its facilitation by the use of word processors and lists the characteristics of good writers, and the development of these by the provision of well-designed word processors. Chapter 9 covers the incorporation of 'intelligence' in software and the design and use of 'intelligent tutoring systems' (ITSs), the characteristics of machine-based intelligent tutors; the 'buggy' system, its problems and alternative approaches to the development of ITSs. Finally, in Chapter 10 the claims made for the use of computers in education are re-evaluated and the distinction between the promise and the reality is drawn. Claims made for the likely benefits of hypermedia systems and problems in their application are discussed.

Acknowledgements

Whilst writing this book, I have had the opportunity to discuss much of the material directly with people in Britain, Canada, the United States, Israel and South Korea. In addition, two UNESCO meetings on informatics and education provided the opportunity to learn of a wide variety of work being carried out throughout the world.

On a personal level, I owe thanks to Irvin Rubincam who not only shared many hours of discussion but who was also instrumental in enabling me to spend two summers at the Ontario Institute for Studies in Education, where I had the opportunity to discuss much of this material with graduate students and colleagues from a wide range of backgrounds. Of these, particular thanks to John MacDonald and Gary Thain who pointed me in the direction of instructional design and its relationship to educational computing, and to Peter Skillen who listened patiently to my reservations about Logo and provided me with convincing counter-arguments from the perspective of a highly computer-literate classroom teacher. Both Irv Rubincam and Peter Skillen commented on earlier drafts of the text, and Betty Collis of the International Committee for Computers in Education provided a detailed review which, I hope, has resulted in a number of significant improvements.

Finally, I would also like to express my appreciation to colleagues and students in the Psychology Department at Hull, and in particular to Andrew Rostron and Robert Ward, whose work has illustrated how the application of a sound psychological approach can result in significant improvements in the use of computers with learning-impaired children.

1 Why use computers in education?

'A modern digital computer is perhaps the most complex toy ever created by man. It can also be as richly interactive as a musical instrument. And it is certainly the most flexible.

(Sloman, 1978)

'The microcomputer is a tool of awesome potency which is making it possible for educational practice to take a giant step backwards into the nineteenth century.

(Chandler, 1984)

How can we reconcile such contrasting views concerning the role of computers in education? Both imply that the computer is a powerful tool and yet the quotations reveal optimism on the one hand and apparently deep pessimism on the other.

Recent years have witnessed what many authorities have heralded as a major development in education, namely the widespread acceptance of a significant role for microcomputers in schools throughout the world. A UNESCO (1986) publication, *Informatics and Education*, documented educational computer applications in some 43 surveyed countries, and a 1989 UNESCO Congress (Education and Informatics: Strengthening International Co-operation) brought together several hundred educationalists from all over the world to Paris to discuss computer applications in education. There is thus every expectation that, for the foreseeable future, computers will play a significant role throughout education.

This expectation stems from a variety of apparently unconnected factors, including governmental pressures and centrally

1

funded programmes, local initiatives involving teacher computer enthusiasts, fear of being overtaken or outstripped by other
nations (national pride), and, not least, by pressures from major
computer manufacturers who perceive the potential financial
gains to be made by persuading teachers and parents that their
children's future lies with the introduction and acceptance of
widescale educational computing. These by no means exhaus-
tive influences also pay lip-service to the belief that computers
offer something new and unique to education: that they
provide, in some way, a cure-all for a wide variety of educational
disorders; that they will provide an insight into both learning
and teaching, will motivate the bored and disillusioned, and will
provide new opportunities for enhancing learning experiences
across the curriculum and across ability and age divides. There is
ample evidence that educational computing has 'come of age'
and has established itself alongside the more traditional areas of
educational endeavour. It has attracted interest from a wide
range of academic fields, for example, education, psychology,
computer science, linguistics, artificial intelligence, as well as
from what might be termed the traditional 'consumers' of
educational computing: educational administrators, teachers,
parents and students of all ages. Given this apparent global
interest, it is inevitable that numerous questions have been
raised concerning the most appropriate roles for computers
within the educational context, and as long ago as 1974, Alan
Ellis commented that 'thinking about computers in education
does not mean thinking about computers, it means thinking
about education', a statement as valid today as it was then.

The educational rationale

It thus seems most appropriate to consider educational
rationales as being central to any discussion concerning
appropriate role(s) for computers in education. Moreover, it is
likely that most teachers, when questioned about the potential
role of computers in the classroom, would require a justification
which served the perceived educational needs of the students in
their charge. If satisfactory answers can be given to the question
'Why should I use a computer in my classroom?' then computers

will continue to play a significant part in education. If satisfactory answers are not forthcoming, then scepticism will increase and computers may well eventually go the way of other much-heralded educational revolutions.

In the United States, Decker Walker (1983), describing himself as a 'hardened veteran of educational revolutions', identified several ways that microcomputers could contribute to education. He envisaged their major contributions in offering the potential for more active involvement with the learning environment; the use of extended sensory and conceptual modes through the variety of ways computers can receive, manipulate and transmit information; a reduction in mental drudgery by the provision of powerful utility programs (word processors, databases, statistics packages, etc.); individually tailored learning responding to learner preferences and performance; more independent learning, and the facility to make one's thoughts come 'alive' on the screen, thereby enhancing abstract thought. Walker placed his comments firmly in an educational context, and concluded that

We have the opportunity to explore a new and very powerful medium of education and expression. How can we let that chance slip away?

Against such a background of positive expectations, many would probably agree that computers can play a valuable role in education – as do children, teachers, parents, books, pencils, paper, play activities, sport, school trips and all the other features found in modern education. To this extent, the computer is now an integral part of the school environment, and indeed of many home environments. However, the quotations at the beginning of this chapter reveal the presence of a widely held belief that the computer offers something different from many other educational technologies and techniques.

Influences

At least three sets of influences can be seen as relevant to the present context of educational computing, namely educational philosophies and practice, cognitive and developmental psychology, and computer sciences. Although superficially these may seem unlikely, and some would say unholy, bedfellows, there is increasing evidence that the coming together of these fields will result in a productive partnership. Educational computing encompasses the relationships between information technology, artificial intelligence and cognitive development, together with a widespread belief that the appropriate application of computer science and technology in the educational sphere lies in its potential to enhance cognition. A similar theme is echoed in Feigenbaum and McCorduck's book (1984) on the Japanese fifth-generation project, where they refer to the potential of computers to act as 'cognitive scuba tanks', i.e., as a means of expanding human cognitive potential, facilitating present cognitive skills and possibly enabling the development of new ones. Unfortunately, this apparent communality of agreement in the cognitive potential inherent in the use of new technology has yet to result in the emergence of a coherent theoretical framework, both to guide research and to enable the more appropriate evaluation of research evidence.

Advantages of computer use

Additional claims made for the potential of computer use in the classroom are based on several fundamental assumptions about the advantages offered by computers. These can be summarized as encapsulating two aspects seen as crucial to effective education: the computer is personal (individual) and it is responsive (interactive).

Individualization of instruction

The advantages of individual or small-group tuition have been recognized in the educational approaches associated with the Ancient Greeks, with the Oxbridge system of teaching through tutorials, and are also supported by recent investigations of the merits of peer interaction and peer tutoring. The significance of the teacher–pupil ratio is also reflected in current debates concerning class size, and by views expressed by some teachers that the provision of a limited number of computers per school will have little immediate effect on classroom practice. Although the question of computer–learner ratio is one which reflects a number of concerns about teacher employment as well as educational philosophies, current indications are that the trend in some cases is towards a situation where some schools may eventually have a computer–pupil ratio which is better than the teacher–pupil ratio. Irrespective of the merits or validity of this scenario, the computer undoubtedly has the capacity to be used individually, a capacity frequently seen as its major advantage, or, preferably, used by small groups where peer interaction, co-operation and discussion can add to the learning experience as well as promoting social interactions. In the latter situation, the computer is being used far more as a tool or resource to promote a range of cognitive activities.

Interactivity

Perhaps the most frequently reported advantage is that computers are potentially interactive and that as a result of this interactivity they can promote more active learning amongst students of all ages and all abilities. The potential of computers to be interactive is important, as, apart from humans, it is the only educational medium which possesses such a potential. A computer is not just a piece of technology for presenting material to be learned, nor is it just a sophisticated means of expression for students, although both of these are roles the computer can play. It is both these and more. With the appropriate software, the computer can analyse student responses and make instant decisions concerning accuracy, style of response, nature of errors and can react according to the needs of individual students on the basis of the responses provided by the students. In other words, the power of the technology is such that it has the potential to act as an individual tutor, responding to differing learner characteristics, thereby providing genuine individualized instruction. The vision implied by this scenario is that students will have the equivalent of their own individual tutor who will be aware of their educational history, their preferred learning styles, their interests and who will provide material best suited to individual needs. Such is the vision. The reality, however, is very different. Provision of such sophisticated educational software requires equally sophisticated models of how learning occurs, the nature of the subject matter, and the interactions between the two.

The computer's (or, more accurately, the program's) capacity to be responsive is important for a number of reasons. Initially, it personalizes the learning environment, and the feedback provided can be supportive both in terms of giving encouragement for correct responses or, more fundamentally, for giving appropriate guidance. Both these features reflect attitudes about the appropriate use in a classroom setting. In the former, the provision of external encouragement for correct responses is indicative of a behaviourist or associationist approach to computer-aided learning, an influence which can be found in the rise and fall of programmed instruction, but which has been resurrected in the guise of drill-and-practice programs. The approach which emphasizes the development of systems which will provide informative guidance represents a much more sophisticated level of computer-mediated learning. Such systems, often referred to as 'intelligent-tutoring systems', must contain sufficient flexibility to permit learner performance and errors to be analysed and remedial action to be taken by the program. These require a detailed understanding of the nature of the task as well as a model of how learning takes place. Such programs seek to act like a sensitive individual human tutor in the nature of the learning activities they promote.

O'Shea and Self (1983) claim that the style of interactive, reactive and intelligent software implied by intelligent tutoring holds the most promise for computer-aided learning. However, just as amongst the claims currently made for educational computing are those which involve issues of cognitive development, so the development of effective intelligent-tutoring systems demands an understanding and analysis of how learning takes place, of what constitutes and contributes to 'intelligent behaviour'. In both instances, psychological models of learning and cognition are relevant.

The social context of educational computing

Although computers are often seen as potentially providing a one-to-one teaching situation, the reality is that the classroom use of computers frequently involves children working with computers in groups. Although the purpose here is often to maximize access to a limited number of computers, the presence of a number of children interacting around a computer offers an important social dimension to educational computing. Here, the computer can act as a stimulus for the discussion and exchange of ideas, often promoting team work as members of the group act collaboratively to solve a problem presented by the computer. Several aspects are relevant to the type of purposeful interaction which may occur around a computer. The existence of a group sharing a common goal or problem can act to promote discussion by group members about the problem. Conventionally, neither individual work nor whole class teaching provides the opportunity for pupils to talk about what they are doing. However, the existence of a small group enhances the probability that meaningful discussion about their work will take place between students.

A second aspect to the existence of group work around a computer relates to co-operation among learners. Bruner (1966) refers to the part language plays in cognitive development and to the existence of 'group reciprocity' in which learning is enhanced by learners seeing each other as equals and sharing in a mutually significant task. Of additional significance here is that in sharing ideas, individuals come to recognize the fact that other members of the group may have opinions which are different from one's own (e.g., they may see alternative solutions to a problem). An awareness of other people's ideas, and the need to elaborate on one's own ideas, can be seen as potentially important components in the development of cognition, as well as potentially fostering a respect for others by breaking down egocentric perspectives (Doise and Mugny, 1984).

The computer as a cognitive tool

Aaron Sloman, a member of Sussex University's Cognitive Science group, has likened the computer to a toy in the nature of the interactions it makes possible. He writes

From early childhood onwards we need to play with toys, be they bricks, dolls, construction kits, paint and brushes, words, nursery rhymes, stories, pencil

and paper, mathematical problems, crossword puzzles, games like chess, musical instruments, theatres, scientific theories, or other people. We need to interact with all these playthings and playmates in order to develop an understanding of ourselves and our environment . . ... The fruitfulness of such play depends on . . . how rich the interaction(s) between player and toy are.
(Sloman, 1978)

Sloman's view is based on the assumption that learning and cognition are influenced by the quality and quantity of our interactions with our immediate environment, and that the computer can be used as a tool to enhance the quality of those interactions. It is thus a perspective which views the technology as a means to an end, with the end being defined in terms of cognitive growth. This is a view to which many would subscribe, but is one which has not always been dominant in either models of learning or in the application of those models to classroom practice. As such, it maintains that the computer is merely a tool, albeit a powerful one, which has the potential to serve educational objectives in a variety of ways. A major use of this tool should be to promote cognitive activity. This cognitive emphasis is also to be found in some of the texts on educational computing. Thus, Seymour Papert's (1980) influential book *Mindstorms* stresses the potential role of computers in the classroom as that of being 'objects to think with'. Papert's advocacy of the computer language Logo as a tool to promote the use of self-directed problem solving activities is a direct commitment to an educational philosophy which embraces exploratory learning and is influenced by Papert's experience of working with the developmental psychologist Piaget in Switzerland. In a similar vein, Alfred Bork (1985), a leading figure in educational computing, has reinforced the view that in considering the place of computers in education we should remember that it is learning rather than technology which should be emphasized. He summarizes his position by stating that

The computer is a means to an end, the end being to assist all students to learn efficiently and effectively. We should make our decisions not on technological grounds but on pedagogical grounds.

In other words, the computer should be a tool which serves our educational objectives.

2 *Technology and Cognition*

Tools for the Mind?

Intelligence is not something we have that is immutable: it is something
we cultivate by operating with a technology, or something we create by
inventing a new technology.

Olson (1976)

The previous chapter drew attention to the fact that a major role
for computers in education is to act as a tool to serve the
interrelated goals of learning, teaching and cognitive growth.
Thus, technology is seen as a tool to promote what we
conventionally think of as 'intelligence' or 'intelligent behaviour'.

The impact of a technology on cognition

At the outset, it is worth considering the essence of Olson's
statement (above) in more detail for, ironically, he was not
writing about computer technology but about the impact of the
development of another technology which was to have major
implications for human thought, the development of a writing
system. Drawing on the work of Havelock (1973), Olson argues
that the development of written language significantly altered
both human culture and, less obviously, human cognition. The
manner in which information is stored and accessed without a
writing system depends largely upon memory and the ability of
individual humans to store, recall and transmit information,
resulting in the development of particular 'oral' forms which
make this task easier. Despite its considerable flexibility and its
impressive achievements, human memory is often essentially

fallible. Details are omitted and biases are introduced. The oral system, although allowing for the development of song, rhyme and tradition, allows little opportunity for permanence and reflection. In contrast, a writing system allows the external recording of ideas, thoughts, emotions and images. Freed from the limitations of memory, the observer can compare different arguments, and can reflect on their implications without the necessity to hold them in memory. Havelock argues

For the first time the governing word ceases to be a vibration heard by the ear and nourished in memory. It becomes a visible artifact . . ... The documented statement, persisting through time unchanged, is to release the human brain from certain formidable burdens of memorization while releasing the energies available for conceptual thought.

Olson maintains that the implications of the development of a writing system were profound. The ability to utilize the new technology was perceived as indicative of 'intelligent' behaviour. Further, the technology made possible the development of new styles of communication. The permanence of the written symbol resulted in the emergence of new forms of philosophy and argument, in which reflection, argument and logic came to play a major role. Olson writes

The process of formulating statements and deriving their implications, testing or examining the truth value of those implications and using the results to revise or generalize the original assertion, is not only a characterization of the philosophical methods of the empiricist philosophers, but also a characterization of the methods of deductive empirical science.

His argument is that the invention of the symbol system of writing enabled many things, amongst the most significant of which was the value we now place on the cognitive processes involving reflection, rational thought, abstract thinking and logic. It can be argued that without the development of a permanent symbol system, such as writing, such cognitive activities would not have come to dominate our interpretation of 'intelligence'.

The concept of 'intelligence'

What determines our everyday conception of 'intelligent behaviour' is partly determined by the extent to which individuals can cope with the demands of their environment. This does not just include what are often called 'life skills', but also incorporates the notion of the cognitive demands our environment places upon us or might, conceivably, place upon us. Thus, the history of mental testing, in a sense, was preoccupied with predicting the extent to which individuals could cope with particular intellectual environments. This places intelligence within a cultural framework. The way we regard intelligent behaviour has to be specified within the context of the culture in which it is operating. What we require from children performing intelligence tests frequently reflects a competence with values and artifacts defined by a particular society. If we attempt to assess intelligence by performance in an environment which is at odds with an individual's experience, then our interpretation of that performance may not reflect the individual's potential level of ability. Our evaluation of competence depends on our ability to match the learner with the environment. If we fail to do that, we introduce a disruptive factor into our assessments, as we cannot be sure whether any difficulties of performance are due to an underlying general problem, inherent to the learner, or to factors within the testing situation and task structure.

Technology as a mediating factor

Intelligence, however, is more than the ability to deal with particular environments. The environment itself places demands upon individuals and offers possibilities for action. These possibilities and demands operate in both the short and long term. There are immediate impacts in coming to terms with any changes in the environment. Equally important are the long-term changes brought about by technological change. The development of a writing system opened up new possibilities and made new demands. The consequences of that technological change have had a significant impact on the development of human thought, and on our interpretation of what constitutes intelligent behaviour. What the mind can do depends upon the environment in which it operates, upon those devices provided by the environment. In other words, it depends, in part, upon the technology which mediates between individuals and their environments. Olson summarizes his argument by stating that

The expressions of a culture – its technologies, symbols and artifacts – mediate between man and nature. They provide the means for the achievement of practical ends, they serve as instruments for the exploration of reality, and perhaps most importantly, they provide the mental apparatus for intelligently transcending the limitations and bias of personal, private experience.

This view can be summarized be saying that the role of technology is to act as both an extension of, and a stimulus to, human cognition. This is a viewpoint which has particular significance for our perceptions of the potential impact of computer-mediated learning. The computer is an important piece of technology which is now commonplace in classrooms and homes around the world. It is fair to state, however, that we do not yet know what its likely impact on learning will be.

What role for computers?

To date, the dominant role for computers in the classroom has been as an aid to traditional teaching and to traditional curricula. However, there have been vociferous claims that computers can be used to enable new ways of learning and teaching. Papert (1980) has visualized a role for the computer as breaking down the barriers that frequently exist between differing areas of the curriculum; as revolutionizing the nature of learning, and as lowering the threshold of the abstract. This latter claim of Papert's is of particular significance, as it implies that computers can play a cognitive role; can influence our perceptions of what constitutes intelligence, and our conceptions of what children can and cannot do. Indeed, a dominant feature of Papert's approach is that by harnessing the power and flexibility of computer technology we can liberate children's thinking and thereby gain new insights into their capabilities. Other writers have gone further, and speculated on the potential of the technology for changing our conception of intelligence. Feigenbaum and McCorduck (1984) referred to the potential of modern computers to act as 'cognitive scuba tanks', a somewhat fanciful analogy but one with the clear implication that work in artificial intelligence could result in the amplification of human intellec-

tual potential. Roy Pea (1985) has also argued that the integration of human and computer intelligence could radically extend
and alter 'what we think of as human imagination, intelligence,
problem-solving skills, and memory'.

These are not minor claims about the potential impact and
implied usage of the technology! They address the very nature
of the development of intellectual skills, with significant implications for our understanding of the development of cognition should the claims be valid. Already, in the rush of
enthusiasm to place computers in schools, we have witnessed
the introduction of programs which make little use of the
technology's potential interactive qualities and flexibility. Programs have been developed which critics claim have emphasized
an educational philosophy more in tune with Victorian schools
than with those of the late twentieth century. Clearly, the
proponents of the liberating potential of computers in education
do not fall into that category, but they are equally enthusiastic
and advocate their position with a missionary zeal, all too rarely
based on objective evaluation. There is no doubt that computers
can provide young children with experiences they would not
normally have; that they open up new possibilities for symbol
manipulation and exploration; that they can provide powerful
environments for producing impressive textual, graphical and
musical creations. However, as Weizenbaum (1976) points out

. . . in our enthusiasm to do what is possible we neglect to ask whether we
should.

This raises the issue of whether in our enthusiasm to open up
new possibilities, we overlook and neglect essential components
of child development. Zajonc (1984) expresses his reservations
thus

We are used to hearing complaints about computers replacing the teacher. As
serious as this is, my primary concern is that the computer may replace the
growing child.

Human or computer 'intelligence'?

It is worth considering the nature of Zajonc's reservations,
because they reflect a view expressed by many teachers,

particularly those responsible for younger children. In addressing this issue – the broad role of computers in education – Zajonc points out that

. . . any such set of questions must be based, explicitly or implicitly, on one's view of the child and its maturation, emotional and volitional as well as intellectual.

He thus places the role of technology within a framework of child development. The theoretical model Zajonc draws upon to support his position is that of Piaget and his model of intellectual growth through stages via the interrelated cognitive processes of assimilation, accommodation and equilibration (see Chapter 4 for a discussion of Piagetian theory). The question, however, is not one of whether, by using computers, we *can* accelerate progression through the stages, bringing the child to a more advanced level at an earlier age than would be the case using conventional methods, but whether we *should*. Zajonc's concern is that

The computer is like a fragmented projection of the human psyche. Each of its functions replaces one of our own.

What Zajonc means by this is that the computer has the potential to replace the mental functions of the growing child; that the development of artificial intelligence systems will result in the child placing an ever-increasing reliance upon external devices, for example, for memory storage, data manipulation and logical thinking. At the press of a few buttons, or by calling up a few operations, children can potentially manipulate data or produce increasingly elaborate (and impressive) images on the screen, without being aware of the 'intelligence' which mediates between their actions and the end product. In other words, there is a concern here that the computer can act to distance us from our actions and their consequences. It, or more accurately the program, is a modern 'black box' whose workings are neither apparent to the individual nor of any concern.

Consider, for example, a music creation package which enables the user to sequence notes, create bars of music, impose different rhythm and sound effects and to manipulate the productions in a variety of ways. With such a system, almost certainly motivating, there is every possibility that users could produce impressive pieces of music. Similarly, with graphics packages, which contain a number of pre-defined images and graphics effects, children can produce creations of apparent artistic merit. The potential of such systems is not under question. However, the question which arises is whether the users will be aware of the processes which went into their products, or whether they will be content to leave the 'intelligence' to the program, and not reflect on why certain consequences followed from certain actions. The speed and flexibility of what might be termed 'intelligent utilities' is such that the use of a trial-and-error approach becomes a readily available option for the user.

There is a very real concern here concerning the double-edged nature of the technology in that performance can be a misleading guide to capacity. We can be misled by the products of the power of technology. When we see an impressive picture created by a child via the medium of a computer graphics package, who or what is responsible for the creativity? Did the child really plan it that way? Was there reflection on how to achieve certain effects or was the picture the result of a random sampling of available effects and a selection of those which looked best? There are very different cognitive processes at work here. In one case, the computer is being used as a tool, with genuine understanding, in the other, the tool is being used in a less perceptive manner; in a sense the locus and control of 'intelligence' has shifted away from the child and towards the program.

The concern here is that the potential power of the technology may distract our attention from what is involved in cognitive development and, in so doing, may result in the provision of computer environments which do not foster cognitive growth.

Empowering environments

John Seely Brown (1985), one of those who perceives the potentially liberating role of computers, is aware of such a danger. He writes

. . . I see potential paradoxes in the very notion of empowering environments for creativity. We must ask ourselves: Will an artistic environment made up of tools so powerful and easy to use, accompanied by techniques so transparent and quickly mastered, really stimulate creativity? . . . designing empowering environments that will entice children into developing their full creative potential, rather than simply mesmerizing them with the ability to produce something flashy easily, will take some care.

Brown's concern is with the nature of 'empowering environments' which he defines as computer environments which can extend children's creative abilities by the provision of powerful computer-based tools. Examples of such 'empowering environments' include painting systems, music creation packages, word processors and open-ended exploratory databases. In each case, the provision of the tool provides the user with a set of computer-based facilities which the user can draw upon in the pursuit of a particular goal. The optimistic view of the use of such tools is that they make easier the task of communicating ideas, conjectures, intentions etc.; that they can act to liberate human intelligence. The paradox is that the provision of such powerful supportive tools may, in fact, take the intelligence and creativity away from the user. In order to resolve this paradox, it is necessary to draw a critical distinction between the *process* of cognition and the *product*. The products of cognition are the observable results of some activity; a painting, a poem, a piece of prose, the answers to a set of mathematics problems. The processes of cognition are the usually unobserved cognitive events which result in the products. Generally, we infer the presence of process understanding through the demonstration and existence of products, and examination of the products can indicate whether learners have mastered essential processes. Broadly speaking, a product-orientated approach is mainly concerned with observable performances, whereas a process-orientated approach deals with the nature of the cognition involved. In many senses, this distinction also reflects that which exists between behaviourist and cognitive approaches within psychology. Frequently, the distinction between process and product becomes blurred, as the presence of certain conceptual understandings can be inferred from a behavioural performance. However, where the distinction becomes important is in situations where

1. The performance cannot be expressed because of intervening difficulties but the process (understanding) is present. The

optimistic view of empowering environments provides illustrations of this aspect. A similar perspective can be found in the use of technology with many communication-impaired individuals, where cognitive skills have been present, but unexpressed because of the nature of the disability.
2. Mediating influences act between the individual and the performance, and give the impression that the processes are present, when, in fact, understanding may be absent. The concern here is that technology can act to subvert or to usurp human learning.

We thus have two apparently contradictory views, both expressed within the context of identical computer-based environments. However, it can be argued that this contradiction is only superficial, as fundamentally, they reflect two non-contradictory properties of any helpful device, aid or prosthetic. On the one hand, using a device to replace, enable or enhance aspects of human performance may allow a human user a greater freedom to carry out higher-level activities. On the other hand, overdependence on an artificial aid can bring about a deterioration or weakening of those human faculties which it emulates. Within the cognitive domain, the use of the technology to replace or to extend certain aspects of human performance – a cognitive prop – can be liberating or empowering, or in some cases, stultifying. What is required is a perspective which identifies those aspects of cognitive growth which optimize the probability that genuine empowering possibilities are achieved; that computer technology is used to enhance cognition rather than to replace it.

Cognitive struggle

The theory of cognitive growth developed by the Russian psychologist Vygotsky (1978) has considerable implications here. Vygotsky has argued that at different points of cognitive growth there exists what is called a 'zone of proximal development' (ZPD), a point at which a child has partly mastered a skill but can act more effectively with the assistance of a more skilled adult or peer. The point is that children can be helped to pass through the zone of proximal development by the provision of a suitable socio-cultural environment. Vygotsky has argued that

> . . . instruction is only good when it proceeds ahead of development. It then awakens and rouses to life those functions which are in a stage of maturing, which lie in the zone of proximal development.

Although Vygotsky's model is usually taken to apply to the role of the teacher in the educational process, one implication which can be drawn is that intelligent computer systems have the potential to aid the child to pass through the ZPD.

Educational situations that stimulate learning and cognitive growth tend to involve a degree of what might be termed 'cognitive struggle'. In Piagetian terms, the learner 'struggles' to absorb (assimilate) dissonant information into existing mental models (schemata), and the resulting cognitive uncertainty (disequilibrium) results in a modification (accommodation) of previous understanding. Where John Seely Brown raises the issue of the potential ease of use of powerful systems and their potential to subvert intelligent behaviour he writes

> . . . is the true struggle for self-expression not just one of mastering the tool, but rather what one wants to 'say' through the work of mastering the tool?

In a footnote to his article, he indicates that struggle, in the sense of applying effort, is essential to learning. Cognitive struggle implies an effort to extract meaning from the information or a situation. The related concepts of cognitive action and interaction, common to most theories of cognition, lend additional weight to such an interpretation. In essence, the struggle is an attempt to resolve a contradiction which exists between the individual's current level of understanding and the presence of additional information. The potential of an empowering tool comes not from using the tool, but from the struggle involved in mastering the tool in order to use it to attain personal goals. When we provide empowering environments, if we are interested in the underlying learning and cognition, then we should ensure that we not only enable performance – that the user is not just able to produce effects that resemble intelligence – but that we also engender and develop the required accompanying cognitive activities.

The use of powerful computer environments, then, contains

this double-edged feature. If the environments remove cognitive struggle, they may stultify learning. In contrast, such 'subversion' of human ability by technology may be highly desirable in situations where routine or otherwise difficult but non-essential tasks can be delegated to the technology in order to allow human intelligence to concern itself with better things. The nature of 'empowering' is to bring new learning environments within the learner's reach. They do this by making activities cognitively available or accessible and removing irrelevant obstacles from the learner's path. The nature of a stultifying environment is that it removes those 'obstacles' that are the source of learning itself.

The central problem in considering the nature of empowering technology is the way in which computer environments can be designed so as to be effective for learning. The archetypal empowering situation is possibly that of the use of technology to free trapped intelligence as is often the case when technology is used to facilitate communication in the communicatively impaired. However, any use of technology that facilitates cognitive interactions with interesting situations constitutes empowering. Modern computer technology is probably unique in this respect as it offers a great potential to extend the range and nature of the interactions that are available to the learner.

Empowering environments, therefore, should act to engage intellectual activity, to encourage learners to take control of their own learning and to reflect on the consequences of their activities; to reflect on their own thinking. The purpose of empowering environments is to shift the locus of control away from the technology and towards the learner. In terms of a distinction proposed by de Charms (1968), it is possible to envisage empowering environments as enabling learners to be 'origins' rather than 'pawns'. An 'origin' is someone who feels in control of a situation and who pursues self-established and realistic goals. In contrast, 'pawns' feel that someone, or something else, is in control, and do not consider carefully goals in life, nor concern themselves about what can be done to further success. What is involved here is the potential of empowering environments to facilitate the development of 'origin-like' behaviour and, in so doing to help encourage what is frequently called metacognition.

Metacognition

Metacognition means thinking about thinking, referring to a knowledge and awareness of one's own cognitive processes. Generally speaking, there appear to be two closely related types of metacognition; knowing about one's own cognition and monitoring and regulating cognition. Knowing about cognition, is implied when students are aware of their own cognitive abilities. Thus, students who are liable to be late for appointments but who use diaries to record times of meetings are indicating both an awareness of their own cognitive abilities and utilizing a strategy to make them more efficient. Being aware of one's own cognitive strengths and weaknesses constitutes a metacognitive skill.

The second type of metacognition – thinking that monitors and regulates thinking – refers to activities students engage in while performing tasks. Very often, we are not aware of such self-regulating activities. So, for example, good readers may be unaware that they are monitoring text until they come across an unknown word, a misprint or a piece of text which does not appear to follow from earlier material. At this point, good readers may well re-read material or look up an unknown word in a dictionary. Their metacognitive self-monitoring and self-regulation allows them to maintain a watch on a cognitive process and to take appropriate action in situations where problems arise.

Metacognitive skills are not subject specific. They cut across domains, and include such activities as planning, self-monitoring and learning how to learn. The growing interest in such skills reflects the shift which has occurred away from product-orientated approaches to learning towards approaches where there is an emphasis on how to learn (process).

It is within the general context of metacognition that the potential of computer-based empowering environments resides, i.e., in their ability to stimulate reflection on the nature of one's own thinking. Empowering environments do not lead simply to the development of a narrow band of specialized skills (ironically, many computer-based approaches do deal with narrow specializations), they are environments which

. . . help students discover knowledge about knowledge, thereby setting the stage for acquiring truly domain-independent skills, such as how to reflect on the knowledge they already have, and to identify the causes underlying the mistakes they make.

(Brown, 1985).

Such skills imply a broadening of scope, rather than a narrowing.

How, then, might such skills be attained through the medium of empowering environments? It is again appropriate to refer to the work of John Seely Brown to gain an idea of what such environments might be like. It has been argued that an important component in the development of good cognitive skills is the acquisition and use of metacognition, i.e., the ability to reflect on the nature of one's own thinking. However, the nature of thought is such that this is, inevitably, a difficult process. What is required is a means by which we can, in a sense, see our thoughts in action and replay those thoughts for reflection. One of the powerful features of computer technology is its ability to record, store and play back every key press. To some, this is a source of potential threat. However, it is also a source of considerable cognitive potential. For around twenty years, we have been encouraging teachers and educators to emphasize the process and not the product of learning; the understanding and not just the knowledge. And herein lies the real power of computer-based learning environments. The computer can record and replay for the learner much of the process underlying the performance. The computer can make available to the learner (and to the teacher or researcher, of course) the series of actions which led to a particular performance. In other words, the technology has the power to reify or to make concrete one's own thinking, and to do so in a manner that has never before been possible.

The reification of thinking

This is such an important point that it is worth considering an example to illustrate what is involved. Brown describes a system called 'Algebra Land' developed in collaboration with some of his colleagues. The purpose of 'Algebra Land' is to help children learn algebra (domain-specific skills) and to incorporate certain metacognitive skills. In essence, the idea is quite simple. The student is presented with an algebraic equation to solve, and is provided with a menu of possible transformations, any one of which can be selected and applied to the equation or any of its subexpressions. Once the student selects a transformation, the necessary calculation is carried out by the program and the derived expression presented on the screen. The student works through the transformations, selecting required operations until a solution to the original equation is achieved. Note that the actual mechanics of calculation are carried out by the system, not the student, but it is the student who selects which operations to use from the menu. The critical point is that each selection is stored, thereby providing an 'audit trail'. This audit trail can be displayed, edited, annotated or replayed, so providing a form of animation of the solution for examination by the learner. In this way, the learner can examine particular selections and see their consequences; for example, selections which led to errors, resulting in back-tracking. Moreover, as a solution in algebra may be attainable via several routes, some more efficient than others, it is possible to present challenges which can help focus the learner's attention on the structure of the task in a search for more efficient problem-solving strategies. The real power comes in replaying the steps and displaying the possible solution spaces on the screen. This is where, in a sense, one's thinking is displayed, made concrete, and where it becomes possible to step back, examine and manipulate the solution space as an object of study in its own right. What began as an algebraic equation becomes a means of examining one's own thinking – a step to reflecting on one's own thinking and developing general purpose metacognitive skills. There is a shift away from the product of obtaining the correct answer towards the process of how that answer might be achieved.

The potential of computers to provide such audit trails or 'cognitive trace systems' is one also raised by Pea (1985) in his article entitled 'Integrating Human and Computer Intelligence'. Like Brown, Pea's vision is that computers can be used to enhance human creativity and intellectual capabilities. His view of the power of trace systems is that they provide tools for encouraging self-reflection, thereby providing a lever for cognitive development. Pea writes

Cognitive trace systems could act as prime movers toward the child's grasp of consciousness in different domains by contributing to the development of this metacognitive knowledge, so important for expertise.

Trace systems or audit trails can thus be used by the learner to help develop an awareness of errors in understanding and to stimulate cognitive reflectivity. Further, the existence of such traces offers an obvious diagnostic tool to the teacher, and could help identify those areas of misconception requiring remedial action.

The ability of computers to store, manipulate and replay information leads to possibilities other than that of the detailed record or audit. It is a common observation that limitations exist in human symbol-manipulative capabilities. Research into memory skills indicate that we are limited in the amount of information we can store or manipulate simultaneously. Work in cognitive psychology has identified many of the limitations of human working-memory and information-processing capacities, and has documented many of the strategies we use to overcome these limitations. In contrast, computers are extremely efficient at storing and manipulating information. Pea argues that an integration of human and computer information-processing capabilities is possible, in which the computer becomes an extension of human cognition by the provision of a set of computational tools. Such tools will bypass the processing limitations of the human information-processing system and will act as cognitive props enabling learners to engage in higher forms of cognitive activity. When we apply this view in the context of young children, it is clear that Pea envisages that the development of such systems will enable children to attain higher levels of thinking.

Acceleration of cognitive development

Setting aside the ethical question of whether it is desirable or justified to accelerate young children towards abstract thinking, whether in so doing we may deprive them of important childhood experiences, we should ask whether it is feasible. Ultimately, the answer lies within our interpretation of cognitive development. The concept of empowering environments casts a new light on models of cognitive growth, models which have been developed in the context of an essentially linear, non-interactive technology. We now have a technology which offers the potential to provide highly interactive learning environments, together with sophisticated tools for achieving particular goals. To date, we have no clear information on whether the provision of such environments will change our conception of intelligence, although we do have speculation. Certainly, the nature of the potential environments is such that they may well change our notions of what learners can or cannot do. There are two aspects to such change.

1. The acceleration of development: the development of intelligence is made more efficient and the course of learning is accelerated.
2. The redefining of the goals of development: the nature of what constitutes intelligent behaviour may be changed because of its socio-cultural context.

If we consider the acceleration of development, it is apparent that this has been a major preoccupation of developmental psychology since Piaget raised the issue of limiting factors determining cognitive growth via his emphasis on clearly defined stages of development.

A body of research has emerged which challenges Piaget's insistence on epigenetic restrictions on the pace of intellectual development. A tradition of research has addressed itself to the problem of socio-cultural factors in cognitive growth and theorists have concerned themselves with the issue of how the growing mind feeds upon the materials with which it is provided by culture. A significant body of work appears to suggest that it is here that the limiting factors lie; that the re-structuring of learning environments can enable the acceleration of cognitive growth. In many cases, performance has been shown to be an inadequate guide to both current and future capacity, and new methods of assessment have created the opportunity for the expression of unsuspected abilities. It is within this context that the introduction of new educational techniques or the use of new technologies implies an improved ability to cultivate intelligence.

Liberation of cognition

This possibility applies whenever a 'cognitively significant' new technology permeates a culture. Cognitive activities previously thought to signify intelligence may become moribund as they are taken over by external processes. At the same time, the human uses these external processes or aids as components in new skills. So, for example, Olson uses the example of the role of a written alphabet which replaced the need for a powerful acoustic memory and which allowed for the enhancement of particular linguistic and logical argument capabilities. The integration of human and computer information-processing systems can be seen in the same light. Humans are limited in symbol-manipulation capacities; computers are less limited. Research in developmental psychology indicates that the limitations of the expression of underlying cognitive skills often lie in the limitations on processing capacities. If we provide support to reduce the demands on human information processing, then higher-order skills can be expressed as the mind is freed to concentrate on the essential demands of the task. Vygotsky (1978) refers to 'external memory aids' such as mathematics and written language which serve as symbol systems extending the range of thought made possible. Many external aids can be seen in the same context; calculators, reference books, databases, etc. They share the common feature that they reduce the immediate cognitive load on the individual and allow for a concentration of cognitive effort on the essential nature of a task. In the same way, the support and guidance of others – teachers, parents, more informed peers – can extend children's problem-solving skills. In Vygotsky's terms, they act to enable a child to pass more rapidly through the zone of proximal development. Computers are now part of our socio-cultural environment. The essence of Pea's argument is that their symbol-manipulation powers can be used to support complex problem solving, that they can become an integral aid to cognition, changing the nature of our conception of intelligence.

There is nothing new in the idea that we can delegate mental processes to technology; writing is the externalisation of certain internal processes, and has had profound consequences. Equally, it is possible that modern technology, together with future developments, may hold considerable significance for our understanding of cognition. Like written text, information technology can function as a substitute for human memory. Unlike written text, however, the computer is not merely a passive store for information. It can be used to structure, organize and interpret the information it is given, and can make our abstract ideas more concrete. Brown writes about a system called 'Annoland' which acts as a form of notepad in which ideas and annotations can be entered. Further annotations can be added resulting in a multi-layered structure. Such a structure is potentially confusing, but 'Annoland' provides an overall view of the structure and of how different annotations link together, providing the learner with a global view of the potential structure of an argument or set of ideas which might otherwise be difficult to envisage, thereby providing learners with an insight into their own thinking.

It is partly the technological facilities for information storage that have determined the nature of our information gathering and information handling skills which now constitute much of our intelligent behaviour. If these functions are in some part taken over by machines, then perhaps mental ability will become more centred on executive processes and high-level problem solving. The broad skills of information management, and such metacognitive skills as planning, monitoring, self-reflection and learning how to learn can be fostered by the provision of suitable empowering environments. An empowering environment extends and enhances current possibilities and performances. It acts as an extension of the human user. What distinguishes computer-based empowering environments from previous developments is the technology's capability to carry out activities which appear 'intelligent', for example, to manipulate and present data in a variety of ways. We have no precedents for predicting what the consequences of these systems might be, as no previous technological development has contained the potential for such cognitive interactivity. As Pea expresses it

The printing press had profound cognitive and social consequences (Eisenstein, 1979), but its effect will not compare with the consequences of interactive information tools that function with the basic currency of human thought processes, the symbol.

3 *Software Styles*

Shifts in the Locus of Control

Introduction

Although the presence of computers in classrooms has been welcomed by many as offering powerful and flexible teaching and learning opportunities, it goes without saying that even the most flexible, powerful and user-friendly of computers requires good quality software if the claimed benefits are to be achieved. Inevitably, what the average classroom teacher wants to know is what the anticipated gains are likely to be from a software package, always recalling that most teachers are pressed for time and resources, and that many have witnessed educational 'revolutions' before. At present, no clear answers exist although many claims have been made. In general, two broad categories of potential gain can, however, be identified.

1. Use of computers will result in improved performances in specific curriculum areas. This approach can be termed a 'product' orientation with an emphasis on the products of curriculum activities, for example, performance in mathematics, science, English, foreign languages, spelling, geography, etc. Applications in this context deal mainly with school curricula as they currently exist, and much software has emerged which targets particular curriculum areas. Use of computers in such a context involves making teaching *as it presently exists* easier, faster or more convenient. In addition to specific subject areas, this can also involve automated

testing, assessment and administration. These latter applications have the potential to release teacher time, thereby raising the possibility of educational gains as a result of an essentially indirect use of computers. So, for example, computers may be used in an administrative context allowing a teacher to spend less time on administrative duties and more time with the children.

2. A second general category concerns the development of more broadly based cognitive skills. Here the emphasis is upon the cognitive processes underlying the performance of particular skills. Abilities involved here include problem solving, thinking skills and such information-handling skills as data collection, analysis and synthesis. Although the application of this more general approach can be utilized with specific skills, for example, in understanding the processes underlying the acquisition of simple arithmetic skills (addition, subtraction, multiplication, division) the emphasis is much more upon the development of a range of general purpose cognitive skills relevant to a number of activities. Possibly the best-known advocate of this approach is Seymour Papert who visualizes the use of computers as leading to the development of cognitive skills across a wide range of curriculum areas, and in developing new and possibly better ways of teaching and learning. Others have also speculated on the potential for computers to act as a 'cognitive prop', releasing children's cognitive potential for higher level thinking.

Although the above represents an over-simplification, many programs designed for educational use target either traditional curriculum areas, or are designed to engage the learner in a wider range of cognitive activities. A question which can be asked is thus 'Is this designed for use in a specific subject area, or does it have a wider range of applicability?' Currently, it is the case that most software falls into the former category, but that an increasing proportion now deals with the development of more general cognitive skills.

To a certain extent, this broad categorisation reflects an 'evolution' in the development of educational software. The rapid introduction of computers into schools created an associ-

ated demand for software. Perhaps inevitably, the first generation of software was produced to support some of the more
firmly established curriculum areas. More recent developments
have seen the emergence of 'content-free' software which seeks
to satisfy some of the requirements of modern curriculum
developments with their emphases on problem solving, creativity and information management.

In addition to the categorization given above, educational
software can also be classified along a dimension which reflects a
shift in the locus of control from program to student. Papert
(1980) writes in terms of a shift from the computer controlling
the child to the child controlling the computer, and O'Shea and
Self (1983) emphasized the distinction between the computer as
a surrogate teacher where the pupil learns by being told, and the
computer as a resource where there is an increased emphasis on
learning by involvement. Rushby (1979) provided a more
detailed framework, identifying four overlapping categories of
educational software which reflect such a shift of locus in which
the initiative shifts from program (computer) control to user
control. These styles are the instructional, where the computer
acts as a teacher; the revelatory, which makes extensive use of
computer-based simulations; the conjectural, which engages
the learner in exploratory activities, and the emancipatory style
where the computer is used as a tool.

Instructional style

In this paradigm, the interactions between the program and the
learner are focused on the subject matter embedded within the
program. What this implies is that the nature of the interactions
between the program and the learner are dependent on the
quality and quantity of information incorporated within the
program. Two forms can be identified.

Drill and practice

This is the mode which has largely dominated computer-
assisted instruction (CAI) in recent years. Its application is easy
and it mimics a tradition of education which goes back many

centuries, namely the use of flash cards and a belief in the principle that repetition and rehearsal will result in a mastery of the subject matter. The basic purpose of drill software is to provide practice, and it achieves this through individualized, self-paced repeated practice of highly structured materials. A not uncommon drill and practice scenario for a young or learning-impaired child might involve the presentation of a number of objects on the screen. The program waits for the child to type in the appropriate number. If the answer is correct, the number might appear, together with additional confirmation in the form of a tick, a smiling face or an extract of music. If incorrect, the user might be urged to try again; a frowning face or a cross might appear, or the correct answer displayed. Although there are variations on this theme, most drill and practice materials share these common characteristics. Despite often being dismissed as trivial, such exercises offer a number of advantages:

1. Ease of use for both learners and teachers. In the early stages of acquiring computer familiarity, it is important that both teacher and learner feel at ease with the equipment and the materials. Introductory software which demands a lengthy familiarization process may well result in a loss of motivation.
2. Use of drill exercises can help develop basic skills through repeated practice. Rehearsal of skills previously acquired can result in these skills becoming 'automatic', for example, instant letter or number recognition. The psychologist and instructional scientist Gagne (1982) emphasizes the import- ance of automaticity when learners need to use low level skills in the performance of more complex activities. So, for example, the higher level skills of reading and mathematics are based on the mastery of such prerequisite skills as letter or number recognition.
3. Individualization: individual access to drill materials enables learners to proceed at their own rate through the material. Although this is a simple form of individualization, the evidence indicates that learners can cover more material (have more practice) using computer drills than in similar non-computer-based activities. Another relatively simple form of individualization is that offered by programs which

address the user by name and which are individualized to the extent of storing previous performance data so that on the next session the individual can be set off at the appropriate level. Such personalization can help enhance perceived 'user friendliness' and motivation.

4. Many learners find drill exercises motivating, although the use of extrinsic rewards like tunes, faces and colourful displays needs to be exercised with caution as there may be situations when such extrinsic rewards may be counter-productive, and where they may distract the learner's attention from the main elements of the task. However, young learners and those suffering from learning difficulties may, in fact, require the presence of such positive rewards in order to help sustain attention on the task, as well as to confirm satisfactory performance.

5. Drill software immediately informs the learner about accuracy of performance. A problem, however, is that if the learner makes an error, drill software typically does not attempt to identify the nature of the error, and so does not provide individualized remedial tuition. For this reason, drill software is probably most appropriate when the learner requires practice on skills already acquired or in the process of being acquired. It should not be regarded as teaching the material in the sense of helping the learner acquire new skills. This latter aspect can, however, be addressed by the tutorial style of software.

Tutorials

Tutorials fall into the instructional paradigm because the initiative of interaction remains mainly within the program which contains the information to be acquired. The aim of a well-designed tutorial is to teach about an area of subject matter in a way similar to a teacher interacting on a one-to-one basis with a student. More sophisticated tutorials use a Socratic style of interaction, where the program guides a learner by means of a carefully designed sequence of questions. In order to achieve this, the program must contain a good 'knowledge' of the information to be acquired, together with questions which limit the available responses so that the program can respond appropriately. Thus, the basic purpose of a tutorial program is to teach knowledge of a topic through a limited dialogue between program and user. It achieves this by having a number of different options available, based on student answers to carefully structured questions.

Tutorials offer the advantage of engaging the student in more active participation than simple drill exercises, although the options available to students might be restricted. This style offers more individualization, so that not only is progress through the material self-paced, but individual learners may follow different routes depending on the answers permitted. There is also more scope for remedial action to be taken in response to individual differences in errors.

Features shared with the drill mode include ease of use, together with immediacy of feedback, although the nature of the feedback is characteristically very different from that provided by drill software. Where an error is made, a tutorial will branch to another part of the program which explains or reviews if the learner's responses indicate misconceptions. In effect what this means is that to be effective a tutorial must contain sufficient information to enable it to respond to the range of errors and confusions likely to be shown by a learner. This implies that a good tutorial will have an internal model or representation not just of the material to be learned, but also of the likely learning strategies and ways in which learners are likely to respond to the material. In practice, few tutorials for school use have achieved this level of sophistication, although progress is being made in the field of 'intelligent tutoring systems' which aim to satisfy the above requirements. At present, however, the 'intelligence' of most tutorials is strictly limited in comparison with a teacher who brings considerable knowledge, experience and intuition to bear in any teaching/learning situation. If computer-based tutorials are to allow learners to engage in extensive, meaningful interactions then the programs must be extensive so that a wide range of interactions is made possible. It should be noted, however, that the limitations of tutorials lie not so much with technological limitations (e.g., need for large memory storage), but with psychological limitations concerning individual differences in learning styles and strategies, and how to incorporate these into computer-based materials.

To be effective, a good tutorial must go beyond informing learners that they are incorrect. They must determine why errors are made, analysing the reasons for the misconceptions resulting in error, so that the program can present remedial information dealing specifically with any errors. In other words, the program must contain a detailed model of the knowledge to be imparted, together with a psychological model of the learner. In reality, few, if any, tutorials have achieved such a sophisticated model of learning.

Revelatory (simulations) style

The purpose of revelatory software is to develop intuition about situations and concepts and to develop the use of problem solving abilities via a discovery/exploratory approach. Simulations are the most common form of revelatory software and offer:

1. A shift in the locus of interaction towards a more active role for the learner.
2. An opportunity for the learner to interact with a simulated representation of some aspect of the world.

The 'world' may be real or it may be imaginary. So, for example, there are simulations which deal with real life events such as emergency action in the event of a major oil spillage, the running of an industrial plant or historical simulations depicting major world events or battles. Other 'realistic' simulations may represent life in the Holy Land at the time of Christ; life as a settler in Canada, or simulations dealing with the decisions to be made in flying a sophisticated modern fighter or as an air traffic controller dealing with aircraft congestion in the skies. One purpose of such simulations is to provide the learner with the opportunity to explore otherwise inaccessible situations. However, it is also important to consider the purpose behind the simulation. If the aim is to provide the learner with information which will later be utilized in a real-life activity then it is important that the simulation be as realistic as possible. It should reflect all the contingencies likely to be found when confronting the activity in 'real life'. The advantage of simulations in such instances is that they enable the learner to experience a variety of realistic situations without risk, allow for experimentation and can highlight the most important features in a situation.

Aims of simulations

In much education, however, the primary aim of simulations is not so much to present a model necessarily based in reality, but to present the learner with a set of challenges and problems which will stimulate active learning through engagement with the material together with a range of problem solving skills. For this reason, many simulations relevant to education may not have a direct basis in reality, although they may well present real life problems. Such simulations may involve being the leader of an imaginary country, responsible for decisions concerning agriculture, food supply, defence, etc. Again, it is important to identify what it is that the simulation is designed to promote. If it is designed to encourage the development of a better under-standing of, for example, some historical event then it is important that accurate information be contained within the simulation. Equally, we should be aware that in simulations relating to politics or economics particular political or economic models will be incorporated. With such simulations, the possi-bility arises that the learner may acquire an 'implicit' message which may not be the original purpose of the exercise. It must be borne in mind that most simulations available for education copy only some aspects of reality. They are limited in the information they contain and, if over-simplified, may result in a misguided impression of real world events or situations. Moreover, simulations apparently designed for use by very young children may, in fact, be counter-productive. Thus, simulations dealing with simple weight or volume concepts – for example, involving represented balance beams or jars contain-ing liquid – can detract from concrete, hands-on experience. With the latter, children benefit from a wider range of sensations than can possibly be incorporated in a computer simulation, and their learning is probably the more effective for such experi-ences. In general, simulations are most appropriate when they present a set of possibilities that the learner would not or could not normally experience. (What this implies is that simulations dealing with the manipulation of concrete objects, as described above, may be relevant for children suffering from motor control problems, whereas they are less relevant for children with good motor control.)

Benefits of simulations

Setting aside these cautionary considerations, what benefits might accrue from the use of simulations? Two related aspects are relevant. In the first instance, they can help a learner gain a better knowledge and understanding of some aspect of the curriculum which would normally be taught in the conventional manner. So, for example, in the Bartlett Family simulation (Ontario Ministry of Education), children learn about what it was like to be a settler in early Canada; what dangers the settlers faced, what decisions they had to make, and the likely consequences of those decisions. In a similar vein, the Oregon Trail simulation (MECC) depicts life on the Oregon Trail in America in 1847, and 'Viking England' (Fernleaf Educational Software) enables children to experience some of the problems faced as life in Viking Britain. Such simulations can be said to have a specific purpose in that they provide a model of some aspect of the world through which the children learn by exploration, manipulation and hypothesis testing. One purpose is thus the acquisition of knowledge and understanding about a particular subject area.

For many, however, the appeal of simulations lies not just in their ability to model some aspect of the world, but in their potential to engage the learner in a range of problem-solving skills. A characteristic of all simulations is that they present learners with a series of problems. Learners have to make decisions, gather and evaluate information and perceive and analyse the consequences of those decisions. Children thus have to utilize a broad range of skills in dealing with the problems presented, possibly calling on a number of specific abilities to deal with the situations encountered.

The facility of simulations to call upon a wide range of problem-solving abilities has resulted in the 'Adventure Game' format becoming popular in many educational contexts. Here, the child is placed in an imaginary world which may be populated with a range of characters – dwarfs, witches, dragons, wizards, orcs, giants and unicorns to name but a few – as well as containing a number of places to visit and explore; castles, magic lakes, dark forests and mysterious caverns. Inevitably, there is a major challenge to be accomplished – rescuing captured children, finding a magic ring, discovering treasure, defeating the forces of evil – and this challenge can only be successfully accomplished by solving a number of problems *en route*. Such problems revolve around the characters and scenes, but can also require the application of language and memory skills, mathematics, logic, lateral thinking and decision making skills. The 'game' thus becomes a vehicle for children to exercise the abilities acquired in the classroom in the pursuit of personally significant goals, i.e., solving the problems to succeed in the game. The solution of the problems may require work away from the computer involving library searches and other information-gathering activities. In addition, the nature of the problems presented and the solutions required may require children working together in teams to gather the necessary information. In such situations, the 'game' becomes a stimulus for a wide range of other educationally significant activities. The purpose of such adventure games is not the reflection of reality for the purpose of teaching about a real-life situation, rather it is the use of fantasy as a means to encourage the use of a number of cognitive activities. Well designed (i.e., appropriate to the children's abilities) adventure games are widely reported by teachers to be highly motivating.

Active learning through exploration and hypothesis testing, together with the setting of challenges, provides a motivating learning environment. The provision of such an environment carries with it the potential to encourage social interactions to deal with the challenges presented. In addition, individual strategies can be utilized as there is not necessarily a single 'correct' solution. Many simulations provide sufficiently rich environments to enable children to utilize a variety of strategies on a number of occasions, thereby providing the opportunity to experience the consequences of a number of different decisions. The nature of many simulations is such that the problems presented require the use of information acquired away from the computer, thereby offering the opportunity to develop and utilize information-handling skills.

In summary, the advantages of simulations are that they:

1. Allow exploration of otherwise inaccessible situations.
2. Encourage active involvement and discovery learning.
3. Are motivating.
4. Encourage social interactions.
5. Facilitate the use of individual strategies.

Disadvantages of simulations

Amongst the disadvantages are that they can be inappropriately used to offer experiences which would be better provided by concrete experience. Further, complex simulations may be confusing to the child and, in the absence of corrective guidance, the child may lose motivation and interest as a result of the complexity of the simulated environment. In addition, although a simulation may appear to be motivating and to be engaging the child in active exploration, there is no guarantee that learning is taking place. It is always possible that the apparent exploration, hypothesis testing and problem solving are little more than trial and error. This implies an important role for the teacher in monitoring and guiding where appropriate. The further question of whether children transfer the skills utilized in computer-based simulations to non-computer activities is one which has yet to be adequately resolved. Another restriction in simulations is that although they can present linguistically rich descriptions, their language-understanding is restricted, often to only a few hundred words and to simple commands. Linguistically, the emphasis is upon the user's receptive language and frustration can emerge as a result of the limited language understanding capabilities of the program. Although this may encourage the child to think of other ways of expressing wishes or instructions, there is little likelihood in the immediate future that simulations will be able to handle the complexity of language common to everyday use.

Conjectural style

In certain respects, conjectural software shares many similarities with revelatory software. A distinction which can be made is that in revelatory software the emphasis is on some aspect of the simulation being revealed as a result of the learner's exploratory activities. The underlying information is, in essence, hidden from the learner who is required to explore various possibilities in order to discover the information contained within the simulation. Thus, the emphasis is on the learner paying attention to the *output* of the exploration. In conjectural software the emphasis is more upon the nature of the thinking skills and the hypothesis testing encouraged. The software environment becomes a vehicle by which the learners can explore the nature of their own cognitive models; the software becomes a mirror for the learner's cognition. The shift is thus away from the content and towards the cognition, although this distinction may become blurred as simulations can be used to encourage conjecture (e.g., as in the adventure-game format discussed within the revelatory paradigm).

Conjectural microworlds

Conjectural software consists of exploratory activities and games which are intended to be motivating, and which also encourage the development of creativity and problem-solving abilities. Conjectural activities are discovery-orientated, with considerable initiative coming from the learner. In these activities the computer provides a 'microworld' or environment for exploration, testing ideas, forming and evaluating hypotheses and productive play. The nature of these microworlds is such that they are designed to be environments in which interesting things take place as a result of the user's actions/explorations and in which there are interesting and important things to be learned.

An important principle of conjectural-style software is that the user has to initiate action in order to discover more about the microworld. The environment is essentially passive until such time as the child makes an input to which the program can respond. There is thus an emphasis on the child initiating a decision, performing an action and perceiving the consequences of that action. Depending on the nature of the microworld, the actions required can range from simple to complex. Thus, a conjectural microworld for very young or for learning-impaired children may simply consist of a restricted number of options which result in a variety of effects depending on the choice made. Even in such simple situations, the child has to decide which option to exercise and to perceive the cause–effect relationships. More complex conjectural activities might involve the use of simple language to manipulate objects or figures on a screen, use of exploratory language to discover what an imaginary character can do, or may require the use of linguistic and problem-solving skills to create a series of effects on the screen.

Advantages of conjectural microworlds

Central to all these uses is an approach which emphasizes a 'What will happen if I try . . .?' Conjectural activities can thus be seen as essentially hypothesis formation and testing situations, in which learners explore the nature of their own understanding. Like simulations, the environments designed are reported to be motivating; have the potential to encourage social interactions; may require the use of work away from the computer; can facilitate use of individual strategies, and engage the user in a variety of skills and abilities. Those who advocate the use of conjectural activities can be seen as operating within a psychological framework which avers that knowledge and understanding develop through active involvement with a learning environment, and that the essentially passive learning provided by drill approaches is not the best way to encourage cognitive growth.

One of the most enthusiastic and persuasive proponents of this approach is Papert in his advocacy of the computer language Logo. Papert makes a distinction between the child being taught by computers and the child teaching computers to perform personally significant activities.

In many schools today, the phrase 'computer-aided instruction' means making the computer teach the child. One might say the computer is being used to program the child. In my vision, the child programs the computer and, in doing so, both acquires a sense of mastery over a piece of the most modern and powerful technology and establishes an intimate contact with some of the deepest ideas from science, from mathematics, and from the art of intellectual model building. (Papert, 1980).

The medium through which this vision is to be realized is the language Logo, which is easy to use by young children, but which contains features requiring the use of mathematical skills, logical thinking, and the exercise of problem solving. Papert's vision of the use of Logo is a seductive and influential one, and many claims have been made concerning the potential of Logo to motivate and to develop a wide range of cross-curricular skills (e.g., the metacognitive skills of problem solving and procedural thinking). Logo can be placed in the conjectural style, as it is essentially a computer-based environment which has the potential to promote a wide range of cognitive skills via the use of hypothesis formation and testing. Perhaps of equal significance is that although Papert's view has stimulated considerable debate and research, the basis of his approach is rooted in a psychological view of learning which sees development as occurring as a result of direct experience. This view is strongly influenced by the psychological model of Jean Piaget, and is significant as it is one of the few computer-based approaches which calls upon a psychological rationale and justification. Papert would thus seem to be saying that in order to develop effective computer-mediated education, it is necessary to incorporate a model of learning in the design and application processes.

Emancipatory style

The fourth software style categorized by Rushby is the emancipatory paradigm. The basic purpose of this style is the provision of computer tools to help accomplish objectives. Within this paradigm the objective is to reduce the student's workload on certain tasks in order to free the student to concentrate upon more important activities. Examples of this paradigm include word processors, databases, spreadsheets, statistics packages, graphics packages and music processors. All these share the common feature that they make routine tasks easier and/or more convenient, thereby enabling the student to pay full attention to the ultimate goal of the activity. They can thus be seen as a means to a cognitive end. Thus, a statistics package will carry out the time-consuming calculations without removing the need for the student to understand why certain calculations are important, nor what the results imply. Similarly, a graphics or art package allows the student to explore and create effects, without removing the creative element which comes from the user. In both examples, the software is being used as a tool to help the learner accomplish particular objectives. It goes without saying that, like any tool, the use of computer tools requires a period of learning before the tool can be used effectively. Equally, it is often important that the learner should know what his/her objectives are, and why the use of a particular tool may be of assistance. Like any objective, part of the skill is in knowing what tools are appropriate and how to use them in order to attain the goal.

Cognitive 'scuba tanks'

It is very much the emancipatory style that Feigenbaum and McCorduck had in mind when they referred to the potential of computers to act as 'cognitive scuba tanks'. This reflects an increasingly held view that computers can carry out certain tasks more effectively than can humans, and that they can offer possibilities not previously available, for example, the ability to manipulate data, symbols and images very quickly. Used in this sense, computers can become an extension of human cognitive potential in much the same way that previous generations of tools have made certain tasks easier and faster. What distinguishes computer tools in this context is that they are envisioned as being used to extend and develop human cognition, a viewpoint which has profound significance for our assessment of cognitive development. In a thought-provoking article entitled 'Integrating Human and Computer Intelligence' (1985), Roy Pea of the Bank Street College writes

Just as adults have been able to solve complex problems with computers that they were unable to before, so children should be able to go beyond their current developmental capabilities with computer assistance. Human–computer intelligence systems will serve to extend what we think of as human imagination, intelligence, problem solving skills and memory.

The 'emancipation' of writing skills

A good example of the use of an emancipatory style widely utilized within education comes from the use of word processors. Basically, word processors allow for the rapid entry, manipulation and storage of text, and are now standard office equipment. However, word processors are not simply devices suited for use just in an office environment. Many specially designed word processors have found their way into schools, with some being appropriate for use by children as young as 4 or 5. These programs offer a wide range of text manipulation and presentation possibilities but, most significantly, they remove the need for the child laboriously to write and re-write text. Anyone who has observed young children attempting to write short essays of just a few sentences in length will be aware that much of the children's effort goes into letter and word formation. This reduces the ability of young children to concentrate on and develop the theme of the text. Obviously, children have to learn the whereabouts of letters on a computer keyboard (although this can be circumvented for young children by whole word entry from specially adapted keyboards). However, observations of young children show that this task is rapidly learned. Once accomplished, children can then concentrate more on what they wish to write and less on the physical mechanics of writing. Evidence indicates that once children have become familiar with how to use a word processor, they write more and are more motivated to write than when using conventional pencil and paper technology.

Before being carried away with enthusiasm for the use of word processors and other emancipatory software, it is important to raise the question of why we want children to acquire the skills made possible by, for example, word processing. Ultimately, the answer involves a combination of educational, psychological and cognitive justifications. We want children to write because writing is an important component of communication. It makes many things possible, but it also makes certain cognitive demands, for example, planning, revising, awareness of audience. If we wish to encourage children to develop good writing skills, then it is important that we have a model of what makes a good writer in order to evaluate whether word processors can actually assist in the development of good writing skills. Once again, the use of a computer tool to serve educational objectives incorporates broader questions concerning the psychological nature of the activities involved. (Chapter

8 discusses in more detail the potential role of word processors in schools.)

Problems in the use of emancipatory software

The use of emancipatory software can help achieve personal goals and in using such software a wide range of cognitive skills may be involved. The open-ended nature of emancipatory materials is such that they can be used repeatedly, thereby enabling the learner to achieve a range of goals as well as gaining mastery of the tool. However, emancipatory software can be confusing to naïve learners and considerable learning time may be required before it can be used effectively. This potential for confusion, particularly with some of the more sophisticated packages, is such that use of the software may require careful guidance, thereby placing an additional demand on teacher time and resources. In addition, there is no certainty that young learners will perceive that the use of a computer tool can assist them in achieving a personal goal. They may prefer to stick with what they know and with familiar, albeit less effective, tools. Although the optimum use of emancipatory tools is when they are appropriate to support other activities, there is a need to consider carefully the design of the tools and the methodology of their introduction. In general, only as much of the power of the tool as the child requires (or is capable of understanding) should be revealed. The full potential should only become apparent as experience, expertise and confidence in handling the 'lower' levels are gained. Revealing the full 'power' of, for example, a sophisticated word processor may well be too confusing and could overwhelm a naïve learner, resulting in a loss of confidence, motivation and self-esteem. Emancipatory tools have considerable potential, but their use and introduction require careful monitoring.

Extensions of the emancipatory style

This is further highlighted by the likely presence of what are known as 'hypermedia environments', heralded by some as a potential major breakthrough in the educational applications of emancipatory software in the 1990s. These environments offer rapid access to vast amounts of information (often stored on compact disc). Numerous options are available to the user as to which parts of the database to explore, with further possibilities being offered after each decision. In addition, information can be presented in a variety or combination of forms; text, sound, pictures, film. Their appeal lies in the nonlinear manner in which information can be accessed and presented. In addition, decisions about which routes to follow can be left to the individual learners, enabling them to pursue individual interests. Hypermedia environments offer a new style of emancipatory software, blending the potential flexibility of the computer with the power of other communications media (TV, sound, high-quality images). A potential major problem with such environments is their ability to overwhelm the user with information, without the user necessarily being aware of its significance or relevance to particular learning objectives. Such environments are only just becoming available, but it is likely that they will have a major impact on our thinking about the educational applications of computers during the 1990s.

Overview

Four different styles of educational software have been outlined: instructional, revelatory, conjectural and emancipatory. These broad classifications reflect a shift in the degree of control provided by the computer-based environments from program control to user control.

Instructional	Revelatory	Conjectural	Emancipatory
Drill and practice tutorials Limited user control	Simulations	Programming	Databases Word processing Hypermedia Extensive user control

Potential degree of user freedom/initiative

In the instructional paradigm, the initiatives lie mainly with the program, and the implicit philosophy is that the information the students are to acquire can be clearly specified and learned by the transmission and reception of the messages presented. In the revelatory style, there is a view that the learning environment can be designed in such a way as to reduce the gap between what the student already understands and the structure of the material to be mastered. It is assumed that the learner brings some expectations or knowledge to the situation and that this level of understanding will be enhanced by the subsequent interactions between the learner and the program. In a similar vein, the conjectural paradigm stresses the role of the learner in engaging in the interactions, but there is less of an emphasis on the material to be learned than on the type of cognitive activities promoted by the available interactions. In the emancipatory style, initiative resides with the student. Within the limitations set by the program, together with those set by the learner's own level of expertise, the learner is free to use the tool in whatever way seems appropriate.

User freedom

There is a differing emphasis within the four styles on what may be termed 'user freedom'. Drill software has been criticized for its lack of user freedom: the pupil has a very limited choice of action; the environment is generally restrictive; the exercises can become tedious, and little scope is given to what are often seen as the natural learning processes of exploration and discovery. Yet many teachers feel comfortable with the option to use drill materials. Not only that, many young learners also seem comfortable with such activities. I have observed intelligent 6-year-old children from Canada and England work together with considerable enthusiasm through a set of basic arithmetic problems in order to secure the 'reward' of a complex screen display. Here perhaps is one of the dilemmas of many drill exercises. The rewards offered are irrelevant to the activity (extrinsic to the activity), yet by working for the reward the learner gains considerable practice on the task. Unfortunately, many of the basic skills we have to acquire *do* require practice, rehearsal and repetition. Boredom is an inevitable possibility. If we can reduce the potential for boredom by apparently motivating drill, then we should not ignore that possibility. Equally, we should not regard drill materials as a substitute for good teaching. They are a supplement, with a role in certain circumstances. In general, drill materials are appropriate for use in situations requiring intensive practice on a set of essential skills. It should, however, always be borne in mind that, in drill situations, the learner is providing a set of responses to given stimuli. There is little active cognitive engagement with the materials, and, consequently, little new learning is likely to occur.

Further along the continuum of user freedom are those approaches which emphasize a more active role for the learner in interacting with the program materials. These approaches contain the implicit assumption that learning is optimized when active involvement with the learning materials can be encouraged. The dilemma here is that in producing opportunities for learner initiatives there is an increased open-endedness within the learning situations. At the emancipatory end of the continuum lies software where the interactions are completely dependent on user actions. This open-endedness, so attractive to many, also contains its own problems. The software, rather than the learner is the passive recipient under the control of the user's input. The quality of the interactions, particularly in the conjectural and emancipatory paradigms, is dependent on the learner and on the learner's level of understanding and expertise, not to mention motivation and determination. As software offers more freedom to the user, there is a loss of program control, so that any monitoring of progress or difficulty is frequently dependent upon the teacher. There is thus no certainty that learners are acquiring the skills they are supposed to be learning, nor that gains are being made as a result of the interactions, unless such monitoring is built into the software.

This is a dilemma which is not unique to computer-mediated education, but is one which will be familiar to many educationalists. On the one hand we have a view that children require close supervision, direction, guidance and assessment, and at the other extreme we have a view which regards children as the best guides of their own learning. Although these are extremes, they raise important issues in the field of computer-mediated education, based as they are on differing views of learning processes and teaching strategies. A further significant question arises in the context of how best to intervene and to guide children in their computer-based interactions. One solution is to incorporate guidance into the software so that randomness, confusion and lack of progress can be monitored and remedial action called upon from within the software. This is essentially the solution offered by intelligent-tutoring systems, which seek to identify the nature of errors made and to offer remediation. Another possible solution is to provide work cards and targets which enable a learner to progress systematically through the materials to defined end points. Such an approach has been advocated for the introduction and use of Logo, although such structure might also be seen as contrary to the Logo 'philosophy' as advocated by Papert.

Both the above represent partial solutions to the problem of how to optimize learning, and are based on a pragmatic view which sees cognitive growth as coming from a combination of free exploration, defined environments and guided intervention. This represents a practical mid-point between teacher/program control and total pupil freedom. The spirit of discovery and exploration is not removed, but is restricted to a certain extent by providing a structure or framework within which the pupil can operate. Such structure, paradoxically, can offer the child more freedom because it reduces the informational complexity, thereby reducing the potential sources of error and confusion.

Teacher freedom

Although Rushby's basic paradigm offers a useful general framework it overlooks the fact that the way in which a piece of software is used in the classroom is influenced by a number of other factors. One of the most important of these are the influences teachers bring to bear. Differing teachers have differing teaching styles which can interact with a particular piece of software. This can be illustrated by drill software designed to teach such basic concepts as shape, number or colour to learning-impaired students. Such software can be used as it stands, providing repetitive practice on fundamental concepts or it can be used to promote discussion and exploration around the concepts. Such programs can be used as a stimulus to encourage students to find examples of similar concepts in the classroom environment. Thus, instead of simply matching (for example) triangles on a screen, children could be encouraged to find examples of triangles in their own environments. Cognitive theory would suggest that transfer and mastery of the basic concepts would be facilitated by such elaborative activities. In such an example, drill exercises, with apparently little user freedom, become a stimulus to promote exploration and initiative.

In contrast, the exploration of a database, with many possibilities to pursue individual interests, can be severely curtailed when routes are specified with little option for alternatives. In such situations, the style of the software is such that user freedom is possible, but that freedom is restricted by the manner in which the teacher promotes its use, i.e., by providing too much guidance. A further problem arises when the exploratory possibilities exist within the software, but its complexity is such that the teacher does not have the time to explore the educational possibilities and so is forced into using the software in a more restricted manner. Thus, the text manipulation, presentation, planning, and editing possibilities of a word processor may be overlooked in favour of its use as little more than a sophisticated electronic typewriter. Increasingly, the possibilities incorporated into modern software are such that a full appreciation of their possibilities as educational tools requires a considerable investment of time, the very thing that most teachers in my experience do not possess, because of demands from other educational activities.

Learning models

Just as software can be categorized into the sort of groupings discussed in this chapter, so it can be examined with reference to the model of learning espoused by the software. Much educational software contains a model of how learning takes place and what is the most effective way to promote optimum learning. The model is rarely stated, but is implicit in the manner in which the program is structured, the way in which it presents information and handles student inputs and responses. Two broad categories can be identified, reflecting two views about learning and education.

1. The first viewpoint reflects a tradition associated with a 'behaviourist' approach to learning. This views stimulus–response connections as forming the bases of learning. The approach involves analysing the relationship between two external observable events, instructions (stimuli) and performance (responses). The behaviourist tradition regards learning as consisting of the establishment of associations between stimuli and responses. Initially, a range of possible responses is available to the learner (some appropriate, some inappropriate), but through repeated presentations and reinforcements, the learner comes to associate particular responses with particular stimuli. In order to acquire complex behaviours, a method of successive approximations is used in which the learner moves closer to the desired goal, as a result of the appropriate structuring of the learning environment.

   Within this tradition, the learner is viewed as being a relatively passive participant. The important aspects concern the design of the learning environment and the nature of the responses elicited by that environment.

2. In contrast to the behaviourist model are those approaches which emphasize the active role of the learner in processing and understanding information. Such models are subsumed under the general term 'cognitive models' and pay attention to such internal events as motivation, expectation and the role of existing knowledge in interpreting new information. In the cognitive approaches, the emphasis is on what intervenes between the stimulus and the response, i.e., on what goes on inside the learner's head.

Within modern psychology, the cognitive perspective has come to dominate views on cognitive development. However, both these perspectives are relevant for examining the role of computers in education as the potential effectiveness of software can only be properly evaluated when the model of learning adopted by the program is made explicit. The following chapter discusses in more detail the relationship between psychological models of learning and particular paradigms of software.

Summary

There are thus several ways of classifying educational software. It can be categorized according to:

1. The nature of the activities promoted by the software. Relevant considerations include subject specific/product orientated software in contrast to cross-curricular, content free/process orientated materials.
2. The extent to which the software allows scope for student and teacher initiatives as compared to program control.
3. The style of software; instructional, revelatory, conjectural, emancipatory.
4. The model of learning implicit within the software; behaviourist orientated in contrast to a view of learning originating within cognitive psychology.

4 *Software Styles and Theories of Learning*

Introduction

Several quite distinct styles of software have been referred to in the previous chapter. In general, any piece of educational software can be classified as falling into one of a relatively small number of categories, for example, drill and practice, tutorial, simulation (revelatory), conjectural (microworld) and emancipatory (utilities). A distinction which should also be made concerns two of the most commonly used acronyms in educational computing, CAI and CAL. Although often used interchangeably, in the current context they reflect somewhat differing perspectives in the field. CAI (Computer-Assisted Instruction) tends to incorporate approaches which emphasize the role of a program in teaching or directing the learner about a given subject area. In contrast, CAL (Computer-Assisted Learning) reflects a shift of emphasis towards the active role of the student in the learning process.

Such classification paradigms or schemes are not mutually exclusive. Broadly speaking, they all contain a view of how to optimize learning. In general, instructional software dealing with a particular subject area with limited user freedom presents a behaviourist view of cognitive growth. On the other hand, materials designed to allow user exploration and the exercise of metacognitive skills (problem solving, hypothesis testing) have more in common with cognitive perspectives on learning.

In a report prepared for the British Social Science Research

Council, Morley Sage and David Smith (1983) surveyed the state of educational computing in North America and Britain. Whilst identifying a number of application areas, they also bemoaned the fact that theoretical models were not influencing the development of work in the field. By this they implied that theories of human learning were not being utilized in the design, application and evaluation of computer-mediated education. Margaret Bell (1985), in an article in the journal *Educational Technology* emphasized that differing styles of software address differing skill areas and call upon differing theoretical foundations. She argued that such considerations should play an important part in determining and applying evaluation criteria to any piece of educational software. The instructional scientist, Robert Gagne (1982), has discussed the relationships between developments in learning theory and computer-assisted learning, and Thomas Malone (1981) applied a psychological analysis to software in an attempt to identify those factors which enhance the motivational qualities of software.

Alfred Bork (1985), a major contributor to the development of educational computing, has stated that 'interactivity' is a unique potential feature of modern computers. Whilst Bork does not discuss this concept in detail, it is at the heart of many models of cognitive development which emphasize the nature of the interactions between the growing child and the surrounding world. As already indicated, Seymour Papert's vision of the use of Logo is based on his interpretation of Piagetian psychology, and many of the studies investigating the effects of the use of computers draw upon psychological methodologies and models to guide their studies and interpret their results. Not only do those advocating the use of computers in education draw upon psychological models in order to support their views, but those cautious of the wide-scale introduction of the technology also rely on psychological models of cognitive growth to lend weight to their counter arguments (see Zajonc, 1984).

Mills (1985), in one of the few papers drawing attention to the relationships existing between software styles and models of learning, also illustrates that, not only can educational software be categorized according to the degree of user control, but also that particular implementations may be related to differing psychological perspectives on learning, and hence of cognitive development. Although such models are rarely made explicit in educational software, they are nevertheless implicit in many designs. Thus, drill and practice/instructional models can be seen to reflect a behaviourist view of learning, in which the learner is seen as a relatively passive recipient of information, with little attention paid towards internal mental events. At the other end of the continuum lie views of learning which emphasize models of cognitive representation and the learner's active role in processing and personalizing knowledge.

Information and cognition

If we consider the artefacts of information technology – pens, printing presses, books, newspapers, telephones, radios, TV, satellite broadcasting and computer technology – we can identify a characteristic feature which runs through the history of information technology. That feature is the extended availability of information and communication. This introduces a problem which is not one of how the information can be stored, because an increasing amount of information can be stored in a decreasing amount of physical space. Rather, the problem is one of how the information can be structured so that it can be presented to, and utilized by, those who wish to use it. In a world in which information is generated at an increasingly rapid pace it is essential that we develop strategies for organizing and evaluating information so that we can identify the things that matter and those that are irrelevant.

Things that matter

A question arises about what are the 'things that matter'. This shares similarities with Papert's conception of 'powerful ideas', amongst which could be said to be those things that society values. For Papert, the computer offers the potential to act as a

. . . carrier of cultural 'germs' or 'seeds' whose intellectual products will not need technological support once they take root in an actively growing mind.

These 'germs' or 'seeds' are those cognitive skills which are valued by and transmitted via our educational systems. They include the range of curricular activities already taught, but also include cross-curricular and the general-purpose abilities of problem solving, metacognition and of reflecting on the nature of one's own thinking. In other words, one of the functions of educational systems is to transmit the information and under-standing which will prepare the recipients for a lifetime of information usage.

In order to accomplish this, it is necessary to design our curricula with such objectives in mind, and to design our educational materials so that effective learning can take place. There are two aspects to this.

1. As learners/users/recipients of information we need
   (a) to incorporate information into existing levels of know-ledge and understanding;
   (b) to make sense of it;
   (c) to relate it to what we know;
   (d) to relate it to what we would like to know.
2. As designers of information systems and of educational materials, we must also take into account
   (a) how users function;
   (b) how they process information;
   (c) how they learn;
   (d) the nature of the existing knowledge, understanding and cognition they bring to the learning situation.

Thus, in order to design effective educational materials, we need to utilize what we know about learning and cognitive develop-ment. This raises questions concerning how computers can be used effectively in education, and attention has already been drawn to the fact that differing styles of educational software can be linked to differing views of learning, categorized as:

1. A product-orientated approach in which learning is seen as a product of acquiring specific skills. Within this framework come specified objectives, detailed analysis and breakdown of the task requirements, mastery of basic skills as compo-nents of other skills and the perfecting of newly acquired skills. This approach is influenced by behaviourist psycho-

logy and, in particular, by the psychological tradition associated with B. F. Skinner.

2. Learning as a process involving the development of more complex modes of learning. The emphasis here is upon the application of newly acquired skills to specific situations and tasks. This approach derives, in part, from the behaviourist viewpoint but stresses a hierarchical approach in which learning proceeds via the acquisition of increasingly complex structures. Learning is perceived as developing from the bottom up, i.e., that there is a hierarchy from simple to complex within any learning situation. This viewpoint is particularly influenced by Robert Gagne's model of learning and by aspects of Instructional Design Theory (see Reigeluth, 1983).

3. Learning as a process of developing and modifying cognitive structures. These cognitive structures are often referred to as frameworks, scripts or schemata. Within this model, there is an emphasis upon the nature of the interactions between the learner and the learning environment. In addition, this model emphasizes that the learner brings both expectancies and knowledge to the situation which influence the learner's interpretation, processing and retention of new material. There is an assumption that the learner will gain a greater insight by having to reflect on the meaning of the information given, and that more complex forms of understanding will result as a consequence of this cognition.

Although the above models do overlap to a certain extent, they owe their origins to somewhat different perspectives on how learning occurs, and in order to appreciate the significance of these models and their relationship to educational software, it is important to consider the theoretical perspectives which can be linked to their development.

Links between theory and practice

The application of theories of cognitive development to education is a desirable goal, although one beset with problems, many of which relate to the fact that the theories have originated in laboratory studies rather than in classroom settings. This said, however, it must be accepted that inasmuch as education aims to promote learning then we should expect and require models of learning and cognition to have practical implications. A problem here arises from the fact that different theoretical formulations have differing implications for educational practice although all claim to be tackling similar issues. The various viewpoints about the nature of learning have resulted in numerous disputes such as those concerning the relative contributions of environmental and genetic influences in determining intellectual performance (the nature–nurture debate), and the relative merits of rote learning versus learning in a meaningful context. Both of these historically well-investigated fields rely on disparate views of cognitive development, as well as suggesting differences in educational practice. Although these debates go back many years, the issues raised by them have emerged in more recent discussions concerning the relative advantages of drill and practice and exploratory style programs, and in the question of the extent to which modern technology can provide an insight into cognitive functioning. In the latter situation, some of the best known examples fall into the field of special education where technological aids allow handicapped individuals to bypass biologically determined disabilities, thereby permitting the release of 'trapped intelligence' (Weir, 1987). Such work may lead us to reconsider many of our assumptions concerning the nature of intelligence, as well as providing an insight into how technology might be used to facilitate cognitive development. Again, any analysis of the implications of technology in this context requires some understanding and appreciation of the various theoretical frameworks which have been proposed.

Although the name of Piaget is, perhaps, most frequently associated with the influence of psychological theory on education, and is certainly the name most frequently referred to by workers in the field of artificial intelligence and computer applications in education (Rubincam, 1987), it is perhaps more appropriate to begin with approaches originating with the behaviourist or associationist view of learning.

Associationism and education

Twentieth-century applications of learning models can be said to have their roots in the behaviourist school of psychology of the first quarter of the century. Although the experimental origins of behaviourism, with its emphasis on the analysis of observed forms of behaviour, lie with J. B. Watson, the influence of Edward Thorndike was pre-eminent in seeking to apply theory to practice. As a psychologist, Thorndike was reared in a tradition of laboratory study, but he was also committed to the task of applying his laboratory findings to the classroom.

Thorndike's major contribution to the field was the explicit statement of the 'Law of Effect' which held that in any given situation an organism has a number of possible responses, and the action that would be performed depended on the strength of the connection between the situation and the action.

When a modifiable connection between a situation and a response is made and is accompanied or followed by a satisfying state of affairs, that connection's strength is increased. When made and accompanied or followed by an annoying state of affairs, its strength is diminished. (Thorndike, 1913)

Although Thorndike's 'Law of Effect' was based on studies with animals, he believed his learning principles applied to human learning, and that the Law of Effect indicated that practice followed by positive reward was an important way in which learning could be controlled. In 1922 Thorndike argued that the task of education was to strengthen the bonds, or associations, between certain stimulus conditions and desirable responses, a view expounded in his book on the psychology of arithmetic. In order to achieve this, Thorndike emphasized that particular subject areas required detailed analysis in order to determine how to structure precisely the subject matter and to identify those associations which were precursors of more complex activities.

His contribution, particularly in the field of mathematical instruction, was both to focus attention on the content of learning, and to stress the role of practice, repetition and reward in the acquisition of skills. His model thus provided an apparent scientific justification for the experience of many generations of schoolchildren endlessly repeating their tables, or for those who had been forced to learn foreign-language vocabulary without it being placed in a meaningful context. Thorndike's emphasis on drill and practice in mathematics as a mode of promoting more efficient learning diverted attention from a consideration of the general basic principles underlying mathematical ability, features embodied in the more recent 'new maths' with its aim of introducing into the curriculum basic concepts of the subject, such as the properties of the real-number system, logic and set theory. The rationale behind the latter approach is that the calculation skills required for addition, subtraction, etc. should be built on, or at least accompany, a basic understanding of the subject matter. These more recent emphases on the principles underlying computational skills were, in fact, pre-dated by one of Thorndike's contemporary critics who stated that:

The child who can promptly give the answer 12 to 7 + 5 has by no means demonstrated that he knows the combination. He does not 'know' the combination until he understands something of the reason why 7 and 5 is 12; until he can demonstrate to himself and others that 7 and 5 is 12 . . . in a word, until the combination possesses meaning for him.' (Brownell, 1928)

The scenario was thus set for a debate which has continued until the present day concerning the merits of drill and practice and more exploratory based methods of instruction. Many would, however, appear to accept that practice forms an important component of efficient learning, a belief embodied in such precepts as 'practice makes perfect', and the search for better organized, more effective drill methods has continued into the educational computing age.

The Stanford project

The computer gave a fresh impetus to such searches, exemplified by one of the major investigations in the late 1960s into the efficacy of computer-aided instruction. A major project based at Stanford University in California contained many elements of which Thorndike would almost certainly have approved, starting with the basic premise that arithmetic skills were best acquired via practice. The materials developed in this project by Suppes and his colleagues (Suppes and Morningstar,

1969) addressed a wide range of elementary mathematics skills including addition, number concepts, subtraction, equations, multiplication, division, fractions and decimals.

The advantage of the computer was seen as lying in its capacity to tailor drill programs to the ability levels of individual children, and to store detailed data about performance. The project carried out at Stanford University's Institute for Mathematical Studies in the Social Sciences utilized the computer as a basis for providing individual practice on computational skills normally taught to the age ranges 5 to 12. Like earlier work, the Stanford study assumed that practice was essential if children were to master computational tasks. The material presented was highly structured in terms of difficulty, and children spent 5–15 minutes at a computer terminal each day. Computer presentation involved pre-test items, practice, post-tests and revision materials, and children started out at levels of difficulty determined by their individual pre-test scores, thereby ensuring that they only progressed after mastering each level of difficulty. Feedback was provided concerning the correctness of responses and, if an error was made, further attempts were allowed. If the error persisted, or if a child delayed too long before answering, the computer displayed the correct answer and moved on. Thus although individualization of ability was catered for, there was no attempt to identify the nature of errors nor to provide remedial action.

The considerable data amassed during the course of the project indicated that the style of computer-aided instruction adopted seemed to be successful in improving performance. However, more recent analyses suggest that it was the extra practice that led to improvement not the fact that it was computer-initiated, although it should be recognized that practice on a computer can progress at a more rapid rate than pencil and paper practice and involves the teacher in less administrative time. More significantly , the Stanford data show that although the programs could adapt to individual levels of competence, they did not have the hoped-for effect of helping the initially less competent children 'catch up', nor did they result in improvements in all the mathematical concepts introduced, echoing Brownell's criticism. The criticisms levelled against the Stanford work parallel in many ways those which faced the early associationists, some half a century earlier.

Notwithstanding these reservations concerning the nature of drill exercises, the adoption of a behaviourist approach is potentially attractive. When considering a well-designed package such as that developed by Suppes and his collaborators, several positive features emerge:

1. The materials are designed around a highly structured learning environment.
2. Detailed task analysis ensures that there is a careful gradation of difficulty.
3. The use of successive approximations to the end-point or 'goal' behaviour.
4. Availability of detailed, automated record keeping to monitor progress.

As Cynthia Solomon (1986) writes

Suppes's approach is attractive to different people for different reasons. 'Theorists' like it because it has a clear intellectual structure and scientific pedigree. 'Hard-nosed empiricists' like it because its effects can be measured. 'Administrators' like it because its cost structure is clear. 'Teachers' like it because they are free to do other activities.

Thus, Thorndike's significance lies particularly in his influence on the teaching of mathematics, an influence which can be traced down to the Stanford work, to drill-and-practice arithmetic programs, and to such hand-held electronic teaching devices as the Texas Instruments 'Little Professor'.

Although Thorndike emphasized the application of behaviourist theory to a particular subject area, other learning theorists have broadened the area of application across a range of curricular activities. On this broader scale, the impact of B. F. Skinner can be seen to have significantly affected the course of educational instruction.

Skinnerian learning theory: programmed learning

Skinner's approach is a direct descendant of Thorndike's associationism in limiting its area of investigation to overt, directly measurable behaviour, thus avoiding any consideration of internal processes. In this model, any item of behaviour is seen as a response to a stimulus, and the reason why an individual gives a particular response to a stimulus or event is said to be due to the fact that the two were either associated in some way, or because particular responses had been previously rewarded. Internal motivations and volitions are seen as being largely irrelevant to the learning process, which is seen as involving structuring the environment so as to maximize the probability of the desired new behaviour being learnt. Those behaviours or responses which the teacher wishes to encourage are developed by starting with an already established behaviour and working towards the goal by a series of successive approximations – the 'shaping' of behaviour.

This process is based on Skinner's principle of reinforcement, a re-casting of the Law of Effect, which states that behaviour which produces desirable or pleasant effects tends to be repeated, whereas behaviour producing unpleasant effects has a reduced probability of occurrence. For Skinner, the reinforcement of behaviour involved the supplying of those reinforcers or rewards which increased the probability of the desired behaviour being exhibited. Skinner's theory of learning is known as operant conditioning, and, according to Skinner, it is possible to identify a number of stages in learning:

1. The stimulus or situation which faces the learner.
2. The behaviour elicited.
3. The reinforcement which follows this behaviour.

Implications

In the educational context, the task of the teacher or instructional system is to present the stimulus, observe and analyse the response, and reward desired responses. A simple example would be praising correct answers. Such reinforcement is said to strengthen the associations between particular situations and certain responses, so that when next faced with that stimulus the learner is more likely to give the answer which was previously rewarded with praise. Although such situations appear to apply to relatively simple learning, more complex behaviours can be encouraged or shaped by positively reinforcing already learned behaviour which approximates to the desired state, and then gradually only reinforcing successively closer approximations.

The above summary of Skinner's model does scant justice to the wealth of experimental studies which have examined the nature of reinforcement, its frequency and its consequences. However, it can be seen that as an approach to learning it emphasizes structuring the environment so as to encourage learning, but ignores internal mental events which many would argue were essential to a full understanding of the learning process. Notwithstanding this criticism, the Skinnerian model has been influential in the educational sphere with its emphasis on measurable responses, successive approximations to increasingly complex behaviour, and the provision of appropriate reinforcements for desired behaviours.

Criticisms of programmed learning

Perhaps the most obvious example of the influence of Skinnerian psychology can be found in the rise and fall of programmed learning, which derived directly from the basic principles of operant conditioning. Heralded as a panacea for many educational ailments, programmed learning stressed a highly structured, apparently individualized, approach to learning which appeared to offer the potential for learners to proceed at their own pace, gaining mastery of a task through receiving reinforcement at successive levels of learning. Thus programmed learning material was arranged so that the student would take one small step at a time towards the goals, and progression was dependent on mastery of each of those steps.

In the present context, the significance of programmed learning lies not just in its antecedents in associationist and behaviourist approaches to learning, but in its emphasis on the significance of feedback (information about the accuracy or otherwise of responses) and individualization. As O'Shea and Self (1983) point out, these features are 'twin gods much worshipped in the computer-assisted learning literature'. Both these virtues are understandably seen as important in education, and, ironically, it was the failure of many of the programmed learning texts and machines to deal adequately with these issues which led to its fall from grace. Although superficially programmed learning allowed for considerable individualization, the reality was that the standardization of materials provided a learning experience which was the opposite. True, individual students could work through material on their own and at their own pace, but basically learners followed similar paths to similar ends, with the major variation being in the time taken to achieve particular objectives. In other words, there was little scope for the genuine individualization of learning experiences, nor for the fact that similar objectives could be attained via differing routes. Equally, much programmed learning material failed to take into account the possibility of incorrect responses, and the fact that these might indicate that the learner possessed an inappropriate mental model or incorrect understanding of the task. The development of 'branching' programs allowing for error and directing the learner via a different route was an attempt to handle this problem, although still requiring the learner to take routes determined by the program.

Although possessing lofty ideals, the school use of programmed instruction failed to grow through its inability to cope with the type of individualization sought by many teachers, and its failure to deal diagnostically and remedially with incorrect responses. Indeed, the concept of allowing for incorrect responses may be said to be alien to the underlying philosophy of programmed learning as they are indicative of internal cognitive states which are, of course, not within the sphere of investigation dealt with by programmed learning's theoretical background. Further, the insistence of maximizing the probability of obtaining only correct responses is increasingly at odds with recent approaches to educational technology which claim that learning is optimized when individuals explore the reasons for making errors. Such approaches originate from a very different theoretical position.

It is perhaps doubly ironic that the recent enthusiasm for educational and home computing, also seen as the latest cure-all for educational ills, has brought in its wake a rash of programs which are little more than variations on the programmed learning theme. As Chandler (1984) pointed out

Crude behaviourism in a seductive new guise has dominated the educational software market . . . since the appearance of the personal computer in 1975.

By this he is referring to the use of computers as devices for promoting rote learning, repetitions of tasks, and programs which do little more than act as electronic programmed learning texts. What distinguishes some of the more recent descendants of programmed learning and behaviourism from their ancestors is that the latter were at least aware of the theoretical origins of their material and structured the tasks accordingly, with a basic awareness of at least some of the principles of reinforcement. Some so-called educational software which provides more interesting and exciting screen displays when an incorrect answer is given reveal a disturbing lack of awareness of the theoretical origins of the behaviourist approach they are, unconsciously, adopting. With such programs, the danger is that the child who is prone to error receives little, if any, remedial help, and may come to associate the intrinsically more interesting sequence of events with particular erroneous responses, a situation completely at variance with the original formulation of operant conditioning. Although such programs are, fortunately, becoming less common, there are numerous examples of software which adopt a behaviourist approach without being aware of the implications of the theory.

This product-orientated view of the instruction/learning process essentially involves identifying the relationships between two factors; instructional manipulations and observed performance as a result of those manipulations. Within the behaviourist perspective, both are externally observable and measurable events, and the goal of education can be seen as the design of the learning environment in such a manner as directly and predictably to influence student performance. Although this may appear to be a relatively innocuous aim, a major aspect not considered by the approach concerns the nature of the learner's internal processes, for example, existing knowledge, individual differences, learner expectancies and interpretations of both the stimulus material and the perceived outcomes. Such processes cannot be directly observed, but have to be inferred from the learner's behaviour, and over the past quarter of a century, cognitive psychologists have added greatly to our understanding of how humans learn and think.

Cognitive influences

Richard Mayer (1981) has defined cognitive psychology as

The scientific study of human mental processes and memory structures in order to understand behaviour.

Within cognitive psychology, there is an emphasis on human cognition and upon how information is acquired, processed, stored, recalled and used when performing a task. There is an emphasis on mental activity, coupled with a view of humans as active processors of information. In the cognitive perspective, interactions with the environment result in the development of mental representations about the nature of the world. This view can be differentiated from the pure behaviourist perspective in which:

1. There is an emphasis on stimulus–response connections.
2. Mental events and processes are not considered.
3. Learners are regarded as passive, rather than active, in the learning process.

Cognitive learning theory

In recent years a major shift has occurred away from views of learning based on stimulus–response theory towards interpretations emphasizing the role of active, semantic encoding (coding according to meaning). Within this framework there is a sequence of internal processing and information processing. Thus, the stimulation of sensory receptors (dealing with sight, sound, touch, etc.) induces neural activity which is assigned a meaning (e.g., sight of a table, sound of a bell, the feeling of fur) and held in short-term memory store. This 'store' is limited in the amount of material and the duration of time for which information can be held. If forgetting (loss of information) is not to occur, then the information has to be transferred to more permanent storage – known as long-term memory. This is accomplished by rehearsal and further semantic coding. Within long-term memory, information is stored according to meaning in mental representations known as scripts, schemata or frameworks. When new information is processed, existing schemata are activated enabling the new data to be stored in relation to and in the context of existing representations.

The storage of information based on meaning is in either semantic networks or schemata.

Semantic networks

Within a semantic network, relevant items of information are linked together, for example,

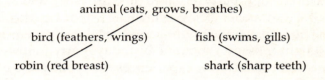

In the above network each item contains additional information. However, using the network, inference is possible. Thus, being told that a newly discovered animal is a fish tells us about its probable properties, that it swims, has gills, is an animal so it eats, grows and breathes. We do not have to be told about these additional properties each time a new item is added, we can infer by using our semantic network. Thus, being told that a 'grok' is a fish, we can answer the question 'Does a grok eat?' In this way, new data can be added to the network (provided that the relevant network is activated), and information can be stored in a very efficient manner. Research within cognitive psychology suggests that humans do store information in this way, with the time taken to respond to a question requiring inference being linked to the number of hypothesized levels within a network. So, in the above example, we would anticipate a more rapid response to the question 'Does an animal grow' than to 'A grok is a fish. Does it grow?'

Schemata

Schemata are packets of knowledge or sets of information which form an organized body of knowledge. Individuals establish and modify their schemata on the basis of experience and interactions with the surrounding world. So, for example, a child may have the following schema about a birthday party to which he/she has been invited. On going to the party, it will be appropriate to take a present and a card for the person whose party it is. At the party there may be party games, food and a birthday cake. Before the cake is sliced, candles on the cake will be lit (the number of candles denoting the age) and will be blown out after the guests have sung 'Happy Birthday To You'. On departure, the guests will be given a small 'party bag' containing a small number of items, piece of cake, candy, balloon. The child's model of a 'party' is based on experience which results in a set of expectancies being established about particular situations. Thus, the above might represent the expectancies that a child might possess about a birthday party. However, the schema is not static. New experiences can modify and enrich the schema. Taking the above example, the party may not be held at the home of the person whose birthday it is. The party may involve a theme, for example, swimming, soccer, disco or a visit to the cinema/theatre. However, certain consistencies will remain and will influence the child's interpretation of the party.

As a result of experience, schemata are modified and become more complex, enabling the individual to generate a set of expectancies about a number of possible situations. These expectancies can be used to guide and predict behaviour in a wide variety of situations. Schemata can thus be seen as integrated bodies of knowledge which:

1. Contain knowledge (information) and rules for using that knowledge.
2. Can contain references to activate other schemata.
3. Can be applicable to very specific or to general situations.
4. Are developed and modified by experience.
5. Can be combined to form higher order schemata.

Much recent work in psychology has supported a model of learning and cognitive development which can be termed 'schematic'. In essence, this is an interactive view of learning in which schemata (including semantic networks) are seen as internal reflections of experience with the real world. Experience of the world results in the modification of these internal structures in line with reality. However, the interpretation of incoming information itself depends upon the structures already present. This is a circular model of learning which sees humans as influencing and being influenced by their environments. Thus, present levels of understanding influence our ability to deal with new information and, simultaneously, that new information possesses the potential to modify the internal models which guide interpretation. Knowledge and understanding are represented within the schemata.

Schema and hypothesis testing

In the sense that this structure is tested and modified by experience, schema theory can be seen as a hypothesis-testing model of learning. This does not necessarily mean that the learner consciously forms, tests and evaluates hypotheses. Since knowledge must be organized (as it serves to plan and control future behaviour) this organization reflects previous experiences and their limitations, and hence has the functional qualities of a hypothesis. For example, at an early stage of language development, many children over-generalize certain language rules (e.g., they put the suffix '-ed' on all verbs to form the past tense, producing errors such as 'goed'). The child can be seen as having a schema or set of rules about language which generate linguistic behaviour. This, in a sense, is an unconscious hypothesis about the rules of language, and this hypothesis is tested and modified on the basis of future interactions with the language environment. The extent to which modification occurs to allow the development of more sophisticated schemata depends upon the quality and quantity of the interactions with the learning environment (this extends beyond school and incorporates the child's social environment). A schema is thus not simply an organization of knowledge, but is also a plan for action – a plan which guides interpretation and behaviour. The extent to which a learner can understand and deal with new information, resulting in the development of more sophisticated schemata depends upon the extent to which new information is structured according to the learner's current level of understanding, a perspective which has significant implications for the design of learning materials.

The cognitive psychologist, Ulrich Neisser (1967), has provided a succinct presentation of schema theory. In discussing perception he says

. . . although perceiving does not change the world, it does change the perceiver (so does action of course). The schema undergoes what Piaget calls 'accommodation', and so does the perceiver. He has become what he is by virtue of what he has perceived and done in the past; he further creates and changes himself by what he perceives and does in the present.

Learning, then, occurs when a learner uses a schema to incorporate and understand information which is at variance with some aspect of the schema itself. In order to incorporate the information, the user must either change the information or must change the schema – accommodation. Robinson (1980) expresses this as follows

Practical activity often has to confront obstacles not conceived of by the thought which initiated the activity. A contradiction arises in which the individual needs to carry out the activity yet lacks the ideas necessary to guide this activity. This contradiction, if it is to be resolved, leads to the development of new ideas.

Humans as information processors

The idea that humans are active processors of information, bringing experience and expectations to new situations and interpreting information in the light of past personal experience, is not a new one. Some of the earliest experimental work which led to the formation of schema theory was carried out by Bartlett (1932) in research on how people remember prose. He presented British students with short stories from North American Indian culture. After one person had read the passage, he wrote down all he could remember. This version was then read by a second person who wrote down all he could recall; this version was passed to another person and so on. As the students were British, they had little familiarity with the ideas in the material (no schema to guide interpretation) and Bartlett was able to document a number of major changes that occurred as attempted recall took place:

1. Omission of details – levelling/flattening.
2. Few distinctive details recalled – sharpening.
3. The passages became more compact and more consistent with expectations – rationalization.

Bartlett's work showed that in storing and recalling information we actively try to assign meaning to the information so that we can incorporate it into existing schemata. What is recalled is a combination of what is presented and the reader's schema into which information is incorporated. New information will only be recalled to the extent that it can be successfully incorporated into existing schemata.

Bartlett's research indicated that humans used their own knowledge and understanding to guide future understanding, i.e., that they were active processors of information. Unfortunately, the significance of his work was under-estimated in the then dominant climate of behaviourism with its stimulus–response view of learning, in which the learner played a passive role.

More recent theoretical formulations have, however, re-emphasized the significance of schema theory for understanding human learning. A significant influence in this has been the work of Jean Piaget who remains a major figure in cognitive and developmental psychology, and is one of the most-quoted authors in the literature on computer-assisted learning and artificial intelligence.

Piagetian theory

The significance of Piaget lies perhaps in two areas: for psychologists it is in his view of the stages of cognitive development; whereas in the field of CAL his model of how knowledge is represented is possibly of more significance.

Piagetian theory consists of an emphasis on internal processing and on how information is represented. Central to the theory are a number of major points:

1. There are continuous and progressive changes in mental structures.
2. These structures appear in a fixed order.
3. Cognitive development is influenced by experience.
4. Cognition originates via a process of internalizing actions.
5. Intelligence increases as thinking is freed from a basis in action and direct perception.
6. Interactions with the world result in the development of mental models – schemata.

In addition, the major processes of assimilation, accommodation and equilibration are regarded as being central to the theory and to cognitive development. 'Assimilation' involves the incorporation of new knowledge into existing mental structures. The complementary process of 'accommodation' describes the modification of those models in order to take account of conflicting information. The central process leading to accommodation is that of equilibration. Piaget postulated that organisms sought to maintain internal stability (equilibrium) when faced with changing circumstances. Changes in the outside world are seen as causing disturbances in internal systems, including cognitive systems. In order to re-establish equilibrium, these internal systems undergo modification (accommodation), resulting in a new and better equilibrium.

Cognitive growth is thus seen as a consequence of humans' internal motivation to seek and establish an understanding of more complex information. Conflict between ideas and ways of thinking will be a significant cause of cognitive growth as they will cause an imbalance which results in conceptual development as the developing mind re-establishes equilibrium. There is thus an emphasis on internal processing, active involvement with the environment and on the activation of an individual's own schemata in order to process and understand new situations.

Modifications to Piagetian theory

In the Piagetian model, development occurs as a progression through a series of stages, each characterized by its own form of equilibration. An essential component in this model is that learning is only possible if a complex structure is based upon a simpler structure, a conclusion which finds echoes in Papert's view of the use of computers in education, and in Gagne's conclusion that learning progresses from the bottom up. This notion – that new learning should be based on existing knowledge and understanding – is one of the most significant features to emerge from Piagetian psychology, yet it appears that the Piagetians themselves occasionally overlooked its significance for the design of studies investigating the validity of the theory. Piaget's view that cognitive growth occurred in stages generated numerous studies investigating the validity, or otherwise, of stage theory. The overall conclusion to emerge was that many Piagetians failed to take account of the child's current mental state and world knowledge, and that they were presented with tasks which could not be assimilated or accommodated within existing schemata. These failings in the design of task situations resulted in an under-estimation of children's mental abilities.

This research tradition, generally associated with the developmental model of Jerome Bruner, has revealed that many of the claims made for the strict interpretation of stage theory are not justified, and that children are often less limited than originally suggested, provided that tasks are presented in such a way that they 'make sense' to the child, i.e., can be processed by existing schemata.

The developments which have occurred within Piagetian theory can be seen as maintaining the emphasis on interaction, active processing and the activation of existing schemata whilst also focusing attention on the importance of design of task structure when seeking to evaluate children's cognitive abilities.

A major emphasis within this framework is upon the development of schemata as a result of the individual's interactions with the world. Ulrich Neisser (1967) refers to the development of schemata through the learner exercising control and influence over the environment and being able to perceive the consequences of that influence, i.e., to link cause and effect. Norman and Rumelhart (1975) categorize three modes of learning:

1. Accretion – the addition of new knowledge to existing schemata.
2. Structuring – the formation of new conceptualizations when existing schemata no longer suffice.
3. Tuning – the fine adjustment of knowledge to a particular task. This occurs when the appropriate schemata exist and the necessary knowledge is within them, but they are insufficient for the task at hand because they are too general or are not matched to the particular task.

In these terms, 'accretion', the most common form of learning, is equivalent to 'assimilation' and 'structuring' to 'accommodation'. A similar point is made by Schank (1982) in his theory of dynamic memory. Based upon his work in artificial intelligence,

Schank uses the term 'script' rather than 'schema' but his general intention is the same. His main point is that simply memorizing is not enough, but that the learner must have a context of meaning into which to place newly presented information in order to make intelligent use of the information. Schank maintains that the most efficient learning occurs when we remind ourselves (or are reminded) of a previous script and we activate and modify it to process new data. This bears close resemblance to Gagne's view of the importance of activating previously acquired knowledge, but also shares similarities with Norman's (1982) argument that knowledge does not imply understanding . The latter comes when the former is interpreted in the light of existing conceptual frameworks and semantic networks.

The views of learning designated here as schematic rely heavily on the hypothesis that schemata develop as a result of direct experience with and of the world. Thus, the quality and quantity of interactions will significantly influence the development of schemata. In addition, the models imply that in order to optimize learning, it is important to take learners' schemata into account.

The significance of 'active' control

The notion of active involvement has often been interpreted as implying direct physical involvement, originating in motor actions in early infancy. Although such direct motor experience is important, the presence of good cognitive skills among individuals who have been physically impaired since birth suggests a modification of such a literal interpretation. Neisser refers to the individual developing schemata through exercising control over the environment and through perceiving the consequences of such control (a factor also linked to intrinsic motivation – see Chapter 5). This does not necessitate conventional physical control, but does imply that the learner perceives the relationships between cause and effect via some system of control. Although this is often motor action, such control can be exercised by other means available to the learner. The important point is that the learner is still exercising control albeit via other systems.

Neisser's statement implies that if individuals can gain control over the immediate environment then schemata can develop. Such control can be exercised by means other than just motor control, and Paul Goldenberg and Sylvia Weir's work using Logo with physically handicapped children illustrates how computer technology can be harnessed to provide an insight into cognitive potential. In these studies, carried out when Weir and Goldenberg were members of the MIT Logo group, severely physically impaired children were given the opportunity to use Logo by means of specially designed control devices (simple switches and button boxes). Observations of the students indicated a much higher degree of intellectual potential than had been revealed by classroom assessments. Weir (1987) referred to this as the 'release of trapped intelligence', implying that the potential had been there but had not been revealed under conventional methodologies. Providing the students with the opportunity to exercise control and to link cause and effect enabled the students to demonstrate the skills and potential that they possessed. The significant point is not that this was revealed through the use of Logo, although this is an important component. It is that the use of Logo in these studies was based on a view that cognitive growth results from active participation with a learning environment – an interaction in which changes initiated by the individual are perceived by that individual and related to existing understanding. This is consistent with both Piaget's view and that outlined by Neisser.

Piaget's 'contribution'

In the present context, Piaget can be seen as having made two important contributions, one positive and one negative. First, he laid the foundation stone of the constructivist, hierarchical model of cognitive growth, later developed by Bruner and by other cognitive psychologists. This approach emphasizes the active role of the learner and the significance of meaningful interactions with the environment (meaningful to the learner's current cognitive level). Second, by making striking claims about children's limitations, Piaget stimulated a research tradition which attacked these assertions by making explicit the limiting factors in the learning process. The work of Bruner and others has clearly demonstrated that the limiting factors have often been in the testing situation and task structure rather than within the learner (see Donaldson, 1978, for an excellent review of such work). It is significant that although Papert acknowledges the influence of Piaget in his work, he writes

Piaget writes about the order in which the child develops different intellectual abilities. I give more weight to the influence of the materials a particular culture provides in determining that order . . .. The Piaget of stage theory is essentially conservative, almost reactionary, in emphasising what children cannot do.

Papert is thus drawing attention to the importance of the nature of the environment in affecting cognition and cognitive growth, a theme which echoes Olson's emphasis on the interaction between technology and cognition.

Implications

The direct implication of the constructivist view of learning for the design of learning experiences is that they should begin with a framework of knowledge with which the learner is familiar, then show parallels between the existing framework and new materials. In addition, the learner should be able to explore the difference between old and new materials, thereby allowing opportunity for accommodation and conceptual restructuring. The notion of schematic development depends upon both the learning environment and upon the present cognitive state of the learner, which defines the operations that can be carried out upon the environment. More accurately, it depends upon a matching of the two. Designing learning materials on this basis implies not only a careful analysis of the task, but also a close attention to individual differences. What a learner gains from a situation depends upon the matching of the task to present schemata: information must be within reach (accessible to) current mental models in order for the individual to act upon and develop the models. In Piaget's terms, accommodation cannot take place unless assimilation can be attempted. The learner must be able to carry out operations on the learning material, but at the same time the activity should serve to display some of the weaknesses of the current level of understanding.

The above is the basis of Papert's advocacy of Logo. Turtle geometry is said to succeed because it can be related to 'body knowledge', i.e., a domain of experience with which the child is familiar and to which the learner can relate. In the Piagetian and constructivist schemes, 'knowing' an object consists of acting upon it, manipulating it and discovering its properties. Note, however, that the 'object' need not necessarily be a physical object. It can, for example, be a linguistic, symbolic or conceptual object in the sense that these can be manipulated and their functions explored. Such 'objects', be they concrete or abstract, become 'objects to think with' as they are the vehicles of cognition. Thus, a programming language represents an 'object to think with' as the user manipulates it and explores its possibilities. Pea (1985) has argued that the symbol-manipulation possibilities inherent in computers offer new possibilities for examining and developing human cognition.

The current discussion has emphasized the active role of the learner in acquiring and developing cognitive skills, and the importance of providing opportunities for meaningful interactions to occur. As indicated above, the provision of objects to think with does not just refer to physical objects, but can also apply to more abstract ideas and concepts which can be manipulated cognitively rather than physically. However, it should also be pointed out that not all learning occurs as a result of direct personal experience. Bandura (1977) has pointed out that learning also occurs as a result of:

1. Interactions with social environments.
2. Observing the behaviour of others and its consequences.

According to Bandura, we often learn from the social context in which we are placed. An important component of this is observational learning where we gain information as a result of observing the behaviour of other individuals in a similar situation. Thus, for example, if we are uncertain about the sequence of actions necessary to use a public telephone in a foreign city, we might take the opportunity to observe someone else using the telephone and then copy the behaviour. This, however, is not simple imitation. It involves activating such schemata as we possess to deal with a given situation and then incorporating the new information into the schemata. The observations will only 'make sense' to the extent that they can be incorporated into existing understanding. The learner or observer is still making the knowledge personal and is thus acting upon the information in an active sense. The observational learning is not passive but is influenced by what the learner wants to know and by what knowledge and understanding is already possessed.

Objects of instruction

Gagne (1970, 1975) referred to the objects which stimulated learning as 'objects of instruction', i.e. stimuli from which concepts could be taught or derived. Gagne's model of learning and instruction is a hierarchical one in which complex cognitive skills are based upon the mastery of simpler skills. In this model, as in Piaget's and Bruner's, the components of cognitive growth are to be found in the child's environment and in the nature of the interactions with the environment.

Children are growing up in a society in which the microcomputer is often one of the 'objects' of instruction or, more flexibly, one of the 'objects to think with'. Sloman (1978) described the modern digital computer as 'perhaps the most complex toy ever invented'. His use of the word 'toy' is particularly apt. As outlined above, cognitive growth can be visualized as a process which is dependent upon the nature of our interactions with the environment. From early childhood, many of these interactions can be viewed as 'play' activities in that they involve manipulations and operations in a creative and open-ended spirit. Out of these interactions comes understanding, i.e., cognition.

Viewed within this framework, the computer is an essentially neutral 'toy'. Its efficiency as a provider of stimuli for encouraging cognitive growth depends significantly on what type of computer-based experiences are provided, how they are structured, on the nature of the interactions they permit, and on the ideas they incorporate.

Two major theoretical perspectives on learning have been outlined – the behaviourist and the cognitive approaches. The distinctive difference between the two concerns the attention paid to internal mental processes, and, hence, to the role of the learner in the learning process. Broadly speaking, this difference reflects a shift in degree of emphasis in which the learner comes to play a more active role in interpreting and acquiring information. This shift parallels that discussed earlier in the context of software styles. The four paradigms outlined – instructional, revelatory, conjectural, and emancipatory – reveal an increasing emphasis on learner control and initiatives. We thus have a continuum in terms of psychological theorizing and a continuum in software styles – both containing particular views of how learning takes place.

Implications for the design of learning materials

The fact that the differing styles can be related to differing perspectives on learning has implications for both the design and the evaluation of computer-mediated learning experiences as the software style adopted implies somewhat different learning objectives. The effectiveness of CAL should be considered in relation to the theoretical perspective adopted (be that implicitly or explicitly stated). Thus, a piece of drill software contains very different objectives from a piece of emancipatory software. In addition, the differing theories have implications for how instruction should be organized.

Behaviourism

The behaviourist perspective on learning can be summarized by stating that learning is an observable change in behaviour, and that stimulus–response connections form the basis of learning. This traditional view has strongly influenced the development of a product-orientated 'systems' approach which concentrates on performance objectives rather than on the mental processes underlying performance. Educational programs developed within this framework characteristically require responses from students which gradually move towards desired learning outcomes. Within this framework, learning is a measurable change in performance. Although this is an apparently non-contentious definition, it possesses clear implications for the design of educational instructional materials. Typically, such materials use:

1. Highly structured learning environments in which the program controls the path(s) of learning; flexibility of learner input is restricted.
2. Detailed task analysis, enabling the task to be broken down into small learning steps.
3. Successive approximations to desired endpoints, usually defined as 'behavioural objectives'.
4. An emphasis on the use of positive extrinsic reinforcement to increase the probability of securing the desired responses to particular stimuli.

This product-orientated view of the instructional process strongly influenced the development of programmed learning in the 1950s and 1960s, and still pervades the field of educational technology in the form of drill and practice and structured tutorials. The promise of behaviourist-influenced CAI was that of 'error-free' learning and individualized instruction. However, the reality fell short of the promise. The type of material which lends itself to the detailed task analysis and highly structured presentation demanded by the product-orientated approach is not typical of many of the materials found within the modern school curriculum with its emphasis on integrated approaches. In addition, there is frequently little attempt at error analysis – the user is regarded as an 'errorful expert' rather than as a naïve learner bringing particular identifiable strategies to bear upon a task. The 'errorful expert' approach is mainly applicable to subject areas where a limited number of learning paths are available; when differences between learners are minimal and when the material is not open to interpretation – in short, for rote learning situations. Increasing technical sophistication in such software (allowing different learning paths, branching on the basis of individual responses) has not affected the fundamental philosophy of the approach, i.e., that learning is a product not a process.

Advantages of drill and practice

Whilst many cognitive psychologists might reject this model as an appropriate paradigm for learning in general, they should not ignore its usefulness in certain learning situations, specifically those in which the rote learning procedure is appropriate. Such situations are those in which the material needs to be over-learned in order to function as an 'automatic' component in some higher level activity. In such cases, the goal of learning is not understanding but rather the ability to perform a function quickly, easily and on demand. Gagne (1982) refers to the development of such subordinate skills as 'automaticity' and gives the examples of the basic procedures involved in reading and arithmetic. In such activities, it is often important to be able to recall and utilize basic elements of a task (e.g., letter/word recognition, simple calculations) in order to allow the individual to concentrate upon the more important aspects of the task. In terms of cognitive load (e.g., in the limited memory capacity of short-term memory) the more tasks can be automatized, the easier it will be for the learner to give full attention to the main task demands. The idea of automatization is further developed by the Russian cyberneticist, Landa (1974, 1982) who perceives such automatization as essential for efficient learning. Mental operations must then be practised to the point at which they become routine. This routine, which no longer requires the same degree of conscious attention, can be used as a 'tool' while the learner's attention is devoted to a higher level problem. As well as becoming 'automatized' in the brain, mental routines can be delegated to technology. It is worth noting that one of the roles advocated for computers is in terms of the computer providing the basic support tools to enable higher-order thinking to take place. Conceptually, this is similar to the notion of automatization, except that in one case it is the human's cognitive skills which are automatized, whereas in the other the technology provides the automaticity.

Those who criticize the use of computers to provide drill and who state that such activities have no place in the modern computer-based curriculum should bear in mind that the utilization of automatic skills plays an important part in the application of higher order skills. Thus, the interpretation of written text in part relies on very rapid letter and word recognition. Interpretation and understanding (based on world knowledge and the use of existing schemata) would be severely restricted without the exercise of such automatic skills. The work of Suppes referred to earlier stands as a clear indication of how modern technology can assist in the development of such skills, demonstrating that the computer-delivery of well-designed drill materials can help students rehearse and perfect basic skills.

Early CAI/CAL implementations were not just influenced by the behaviourist tradition, but were also strongly influenced by the fact that the first computers in schools were relatively low-powered devices. These were restricted in terms of what could be achieved and tended to lend themselves to the structures of linear programs. More recent developments have seen the emergence of low cost machines with considerably greater processing power. This has made possible the development of software which places a greater emphasis on student interactivity and which, as a consequence, lies closer to cognitive views of learning.

Cognitive influences

The cognitive view of learning emphasizes the role that active experiences and interactions have in influencing the development of mental models. Central to this perspective is that learners bring a set of experiences and expectations to a situation and attempt to interpret new information from their own perspective, i.e., 'make sense' of a new situation. The mental models are modified and become more complex on the basis of experience. Thus, learners are perceived as active participants in the learning process, constructing their own mental models, rather than being passive recipients of information. The influence of this perspective on CAL is characterised by:

1. A high degree of learner control over the learning path to be taken – the computer or program provides an environment (often non-judgemental) in which important ideas and principles are embedded.
2. An emphasis on process rather than product; learning is believed to arise organically from the nature of the interactions promoted by both the environment and the user's initiatives
3. Freedom of action and interaction, together with the emphasis on process, is argued to be intrinsically motivating so the need for external reinforcement is minimized.

Within this perspective, there is an emphasis on software which promotes interactivity; enables user initiatives to be taken; encourages hypothesis testing, and which provides feedback meaningful to both the task and to the user. Styles of software which incorporate some of these aspects are simulations (revelatory), problem solving (programming, conjectural software, use of Logo), and emancipatory activities like word processing or the exploration of an educational database.

In general, although software which could be classed as falling within the 'behaviourist' paradigm predominates, many educational theorists and practitioners see the future of CAL as lying with the 'cognitive' or more child-centred approaches. However, what is often neglected is why the cognitive approach might be preferable within the CAL field. The intuitive appeal of such an approach and such software is not sufficient justification for those who would seek to see the widespread adoption of such materials. Consequently, psychological comments on this issue commonly draw upon psychological theories for their justification.

Perhaps the most powerful argument in favour of interactive, learner-controlled software lies in the fact that it is most closely related to the way in which many psychologists see the development of cognition. Concepts such as schemata, semantic networks, assimilation, accommodation and equilibration can be incorporated into learner-centred educational environments, and the appropriate design of such environments should, then, allow for the possibility for these processes to occur. The concept of computer-based 'microworlds' has evolved. Such environments are those in which the learner is free to carry out procedures and operations which in some way embody important ideas and principles. The assumption within such a formulation is that, as a result of carrying out these operations and exploring the possibilities embodied within the environment, both assimilation and accommodation are likely to occur, resulting in the development of more sophisticated mental structures with a parallel increase in understanding.

Freedom vs *control*

Although this is an appealing vision, several problems have emerged as a result of the application of child-centred, exploratory software. Perhaps the major issue is the extent to which 'freedom' is necessary or desirable. A position which maintains that the only true learning is that based on solo discovery seems somewhat artificial and counter-productive. Why should the accidental, fortuitous discovery of an appropriate principle be considered superior to the deliberate provision of support to assist the learner in acquiring mastery of the principle to be learned? Learners cannot be expected to rediscover the past discoveries of mankind spontaneously, and it can, in fact, be argued that the appropriate structuring of learning serves to increase rather than decrease the learner's freedom (Leron, 1985: also see Chapter 6 on Logo). Structure and guidance can serve to provide direction and feedback in an otherwise confusing situation and thus can help develop autonomy rather than restrict it. Guidance, be it from text, teacher or program, can draw attention to relevant aspects, provide feedback about errors, and monitor and encourage progress.

Vygotsky (1978) has introduced to cognitive development the concept of the 'zone of proximal development'. This relates to phases in development when a child has partly mastered a skill but can act more effectively with the support of a more skilled peer or adult (or, by implication, program). The zone of proximal development thus refers to that stage in the development of a skill or ability that lies between the child functioning independently and functioning with support. It is at this stage that guidance and intervention become of particular significance, indicating to the learner the adequacies and inadequacies of current levels of thinking and providing the necessary support to bring the learner to a higher level of understanding. Vygotsky has argued that instruction can play a particularly important role in this process. The notion of discovery learning has thus evolved into the concept of guided discovery learning, in which it is recognized that learning experiences need to be structured but that the emphasis on interactivity and exploration is maintained.

A further problem concerns the nature of interactivity, a

concept commonly associated with CAL and often held to be one of its most significant potential features. Interaction can be seen in any situation involving a cycle of questions, responses and answers. What this omits is any consideration of the learner's actual experience. Interaction implies a meaningful exchange. In a CAL context, an interactive learning environment is one which, by the nature of its responses, promotes information processing (also, assimilation and accommodation). By contrast, a non-interactive learning environment is one which is not accessible to the learner's manipulations, but presents a series of stimuli or responses in a manner which cannot be understood (processed) by the learner. The basis of interactivity in CAL is the extent to which varied activities within the environment give rise to varied and meaningful results. In this context, 'meaningful' refers to the learner's perception of the feedback provided by the program. The feedback must be within the learner's processing capabilities and relevant to the learner's actions otherwise it will not be related to information in existing mental structures.

Conclusion

Several conclusions emerge from this discussion. Although software can be linked to two broad classes of learning paradigms, both contain problems when applied to CAL. The behaviourist style can be seen as being too restrictive on the individual, whereas the cognitive style may be too open-ended on occasions. Further, although software falling within the cognitive paradigm may be seen as preferable because it is closer to current views on learning, the development of such software requires that close attention be given to the structure of the learning environment, the nature of the interactions made possible and the style of feedback provided. This implies that such applications require both a detailed analysis of the task (to design the environment), the interactions (to provide guidance), and the learner (to provide meaningful feedback). In other words, although the cognitive style has the potential to provide genuine individualization of learning, such individualization is difficult to attain.

Moreover, the reality of classroom management is such that rigid pedagogical stances are rarely applied. A good classroom teacher calls upon experience and intuition when dealing with everyday learning situations, and will vary teaching style in accordance with the perceived requirements and objectives. Thus, the type of learning environment which is best suited to assist a learner attain educational goals depends very strongly on the nature of the learner and the learning objectives. Similarly, the various styles of educational software embody differing theoretical assumptions about how learning occurs. Selection of learning materials may not necessarily proceed by evaluation of the general validity or otherwise of these theories. Rather, a pragmatic decision should be made as to which paradigm is most appropriate in a particular context. Where automaticity and the acquisition of well-rehearsed skills are important, a behaviourist approach may be the most suitable. In other situations, involving hypothesis testing, a more exploratory approach may be indicated. An awareness of the potential relationships between CAL styles and cognitive development can assist in identifying the most appropriate materials for achieving educational objectives and for evaluating the effectiveness of those materials. We should also recognize that individual differences in learning styles can also be a deciding factor – some students may respond better to a particular style than to others. In other situations, the use of a particular style may be desirable but not possible because of constraints of time, space, additional resources or classroom arrangements. Ultimately, the goal of much CAL is that of achieving individualization of learning. This vision could not be attained via the behaviourist approach but is, perhaps, closer to attainment by the application of principles derived from cognitive and information processing models of learning. The extent to which the promise can be fulfilled eventually will depend on a closer matching of theory and practice than has so far been achieved.

5 *Motivational Issues in CAL*

Introduction

It was Marshall McLuhan, one of the 'gurus' of the 1960s, who is reported to have said that 'Those who draw a distinction between education and entertainment don't know a thing about either.' Whatever the origin of this statement, there is little doubt that the issue of making learning 'fun' has been given a new impetus by the development of educational software which seeks to achieve particular educational objectives via the use of embellishments designed to making learning more enjoyable. In her book *Children's Minds* Margaret Donaldson (1978) points out that for many learners a change occurs in their attitude towards learning as they progress through the educational system. At the start, children are bright-eyed and enthusiastic – they approach learning with enthusiasm, enjoyment and commitment. As the years pass, many of these children appear to lose that 'joy of learning' which characterized their pre-school and early school years. Education, for many, ceases to be enjoyable. It becomes associated with 'work', not pleasure.

The origins of this transformation have been commented upon by many. Whatever its roots, the fact remains that establishing and maintaining motivation in the school environment does constitute a problem, and the energies of many teachers are often directed towards trying to make their lessons more motivationally appealing. Despite the general feeling that without motivation, learning will inevitably be less efficient, it is also the case that the motivational aspects of instruction have received relatively little attention in the literature on instructional design, with Keller (1983) being one of the few to attempt to develop a practical model of the motivational design of instruction.

Motivation and computer use

One impact of the increasing influence of modern technology in society has been to direct attention towards the issue of motivation within education, and in particular within the context of computer-based education. The origins of this interest lie not within education itself, nor within theories of motivation. Rather, they lie in what can be termed the 'video-arcade phenomenon'. It is apparent that computers and electronic games have strong motivational appeal to many. In their brief treatment of motivation, O'Shea and Self (1983) comment on the fact that use of computers can be an intrinsically motivating activity for many students. Although this may be the case, it could be argued that there is nothing inherently satisfying about using a computer. As indicated earlier, computers are essentially neutral. Their power derives from what can be achieved by using them – in other words, by the nature of the activities they promote. Arguably the most popular use of computers by children has been for playing computer games. When personal computers first became widely available, the bulk of software was of the game type, a situation which has changed little. A visit to any computer outlet, or a brief perusal of one of the many computer magazines available will reveal the vast variety of game software available for a wide range of machines. Students also state that when using a computer at home, the dominant use is for game playing. Clearly, computer and video games have powerful motivational appeal for many individuals.

The apparent enthusiasm, dedication and abilities that many young students bring to computer games has raised a number of concerns among many. Computer-based games have been seen as encouraging social isolation and potentially reducing the amount of time that students give to other activities, both leisure and academic. In addition, there have been reports of what can only be termed 'addiction' to computer games, with players giving disproportionate amounts of both time and money to support their interest or addiction. Moreover, many of the most popular games are often male-orientated and involve a significant aggressive quality. This raises concerns over the equity of access to computers, together with the nature of the implicit messages possibly promoted to young people.

Despite the significance of these issues most observers would agree that there are aspects of computer and video games which make them highly attractive to their users resulting in considerable motivation. The question which has inevitably followed is whether the variables which enhance the appeal of computer games could be incorporated into educational software with the same results. Implicit here is the belief that learning can be fun, and if we make it so, then significant learning gains will follow. In other words, there is an assumption that motivation and learning are linked.

It is easy to appreciate why there should be such an assumption. Many aspects of education revolve around motivational factors. Attempts to make learning activities more 'interesting', to distribute rewards for good performance, and to provide material which accords with learner interests can all be seen as attempts to manipulate the student's motivation to engage in the learning activity in such a way that students are attracted to learning, persevere with tasks and demonstrate a 'positive' attitude to future learning. This, of course, overlooks the possibility that some children's perceptions and expectations of a classroom environment are such that learning is not perceived as potentially enjoyable, despite all attempts to make it so! There is also another potential consideration here. Although the use of computers in the classroom is widely reported to be highly motivating, this might say more about the nature of conventional classroom activities than it does about any possible motivational qualities of computer use. When I asked a group of 10-year-old children to rank using a computer in comparison with other classroom activities, as anticipated, computer use was ranked very highly. However, when the question was modified so that computer use was judged against other valued activities (reading, watching TV, playing with friends, skating, swimming, soccer, dancing and other leisure activities), computer use lost its attractiveness!

Motivational features of software

The motivational qualities apparently contained in much of the computer game software has resulted in developers of educational software attempting to draw on these features in order to enhance the appeal of educational activities. In many instances, the attempts have been little more than presenting drill activities in a 'space invader' format. In other instances, game formats are used which incorporate a variety of curriculum-based activities. In these situations, the paradigm used is often that of the simulation or the 'adventure' game in which learners exercise their skills through a series of problems presented in an imaginary or simulated 'world'.

Whatever approach is used, it is apparent that the use of a game-like context is widely seen as one way of increasing student motivation, with the assumption being that increased motivation will result in better learning, presumably because the learner pays more attention, becomes more actively involved with the material, or has more practice than is available with conventional methods. Underlying this is an implicit belief that educational software can be designed in such a way as to promote learner motivation. This further implies that it is possible to specify those features which make software motivating. Thomas Malone (1981) has contributed most to our understanding of the variables which influence the perceived motivational quality of software. Amongst the factors he identified were the use of audio and visual stimuli; the presence of variable levels of difficulty; the use of fantasy; a scoring facility, and user control.

1. *Audio and visual stimuli*   One feature of modern computers is that they can provide a range of additional stimuli in response to a user's actions. Often known as 'bells and whistles' these include dramatic screen displays, sophisticated graphics, extracts of tunes and synthetic speech. Sound effects may also accompany a program, often to the annoyance of those not using it. The various forms that audio and visual stimuli can take may serve to attract and maintain attention, provide information about performance and, potentially, distract the student from the main task.

2. *Increasing levels of difficulty*   Many computer-game-like activities offer a range of difficulty. The user may be given the opportunity to select a given level at the beginning of the program, or, alternatively, the program may move the player to the next level once a satisfactory level of performance has been demonstrated in the preceding level. Note that in the latter case, the control over promotion (or demotion) resides with the program, whereas in the former case, the learner selects the appropriate level.

3. *Fantasy elements*   Most popular games invoke a strong fantasy theme. The player is an explorer, the defender of a space station, the pilot of an aircraft, the coach/manager of a football team, the manager of a small store, etc. and has to carry out a set of activities relevant to the fantasy environment.

4. *Scoring facility*   This is a major component of most games. The scores can be presented as percentages (e.g., 'You have completed 20% of this level/game'), or may be presented as a single score. Many games also include a 'Hall of Fame' which lists the top 10 scores. Two assumptions lie behind the provision of a scoring facility. The first is that knowledge of personal performance is motivating in that it provides information about personal achievement. The second assumption, however, relates to the 'Hall of Fame' facility and is less obvious. The assumption here is that there is a motivational quality to seeing one's score against other scores. Although this may indeed be motivational for proficient players, those who are less proficient may experience considerable frustration if they fail to achieve a 'top ten' rating, with a possible loss of motivation. In other words, a facility designed to be motivating may lose its motivational quality in certain situations.

5. *Player in control*   With most computer games, the player has a certain freedom of action. Although this was limited in the first generation of games, recent developments often provide the user considerable freedom of choice within the game environment.

Many currently popular computer games combine all the above elements, and there is little doubt that, for many young people (mainly males) the end products possess very powerful motivational qualities.

Extrinsic and intrinsic motivation

An important distinction to make is that which exists between extrinsic and intrinsic motivation. The assumption within much software is that the activity is rewarding (positive reinforcement) and that this adds to the motivational qualities. Extrinsic motivation comes from reinforcement that is unrelated to the task whereas intrinsic motivation refers to engagement in the activity for its own sake – the reinforcement comes from carrying out the activity, not from securing some sort of external reward. Activities are perceived as being intrinsically motivating to the extent that they engage us in a process of seeking to solve problems whose solution demands the use of effort and personal skills. Generally speaking, most theorists see intrinsic motivation as being essentially more productive in terms of future learning and commitment to a task. However, it would have to be stated that many of our educational activities do make use of extrinsic reinforcement. Thus, stars, merit badges, points, etc., are awarded for good performance. These are rewards which are not inherently related to a particular task, as they could be awarded for good performance on any task. The assumption is that children will work harder to secure such external rewards, and that their receipt will result in additional motivation to maintain the behaviour in the future. Such reinforcements are also often incorporated into educational software, for example, use of smiling faces, tunes and graphic displays.

Operant conditioning and the theory of extrinsic motivation

It is possible to find a theoretical justification for the use of extrinsic reinforcers within the behaviourist approach to learning and, specifically, in the field of operant conditioning. The theoretical basis of the use of extrinsic reinforcers lies in the field of behaviourist psychology. Their use dates back to Thorndike and Skinner and the Law of Effect which maintained that the use of an external reinforcer resulted in a strengthening of the associations between a stimulus and a response. The theory maintains that the strength of the association is automatically increased each time the response is rewarded.

The behaviourist approach to learning and to the use and scheduling of reinforcement has been developed within the field of operant conditioning theory which has investigated the use of reinforcers and their effects. Briefly, operant conditioning theory assumes that behaviour is largely determined and controlled by its consequences. Whenever a particular behaviour is positively rewarded, the probability of its being repeated will increase relative to a non-rewarded situation. The vast amount of research on operant conditioning principles (mainly using animals as subjects) has added to this simple picture. So, for example, it has been found that varying the probability of reward can influence the persistence of a behaviour in a predictable manner, for example, use of a variable-ratio schedule (providing the reward in a non-predictable manner) results in a lengthy maintenance of the behaviour. Once reinforcement is withdrawn, the behaviour moves back towards its original base line – the speed of return being partly determined by the type of reinforcement schedule used. Numerous studies have supported the basic findings on the efficiency of operant techniques in influencing behaviour in laboratory animals. These findings have been extended to human behaviour and the use of external rewards of the type often used in educational software can be seen in this context. In this model, there is little need for the learner to be actively aware of or to interpret the situation. It will be apparent that many classroom activities and much educational software appears to make use of such a paradigm.

When positive reinforcement loses its power

Despite the considerable laboratory support for conditioning principles, a growing body of evidence casts doubt upon the all-embracing nature of the observations. So, for example, it has been reported that under certain circumstances the removal of extrinsic reinforcement has resulted in the behaviour declining to a level *below* its original baseline. Typically, such studies involve observing subjects on a task in order to establish a baseline. In the second stage, subjects are given an extrinsic reward such as sweets or money for carrying out the task. Then, in the third stage, the subjects are observed on the task but no reward is offered. During this final 'free play' period, the behaviour under observation often drops to a point below its original level. In other words, removal of the extrinsic reinforcer can result in a decline in intrinsic motivation or desire to carry out the task.

Such an observation is not an isolated incident. A number of researchers have commented upon the potentially deleterious consequences that the use of extrinsic reinforcement may have on intrinsic motivation. These are findings which give rise for concern because of the widespread use of extrinsic reinforcers within educational contexts. There is, however, a paradox here. Children do appear to respond to the use of extrinsic rewards – many are apparently motivated by the goal of securing rewards which are superficially unrelated to the task. This perhaps applies particularly to young learners or to those experiencing some form of learning difficulty. It might also apply in situations where it is important that the learner gain considerable practice on an activity in order to automatize it so that it can be used as a component in a higher order skill. The use of extrinsic rewards can be appropriate in such situations as they can add to the general interest of what might otherwise be a relatively boring activity. Such considerations apply to situations where the extrinsic motivator is not predictable. Young learners often appear to be motivated by situations where they cannot predict with certainty what the reward will be. In general, most software using extrinsic reinforcers makes use of consistent rewards. However, some software, although using external rewards, incorporates an element of uncertainty. This may simply involve variable messages such as 'Well done!', 'Right again', 'You're in good form today'. More motivating however, seems to be material using rewards which have the potential to engage the learner more actively. So, for example, one program presents basic arithmetic problems but provides the reward of a dotted outline of one of several possible shapes on the screen. The child can then join the dots to produce the picture which can then be dumped to a printer. In this program, there is considerable use of external rewards (the pictures are totally unrelated to the task). From one theoretical perspective, such a program should be counter-productive. However, young children appear to find it highly motivating. Interactions between children using this program indicate that they are fully aware that they are working for the reward, but that a particularly satisfying aspect comes from the uncertainty of which set of dots will appear, and then the satisfaction of predicting and recognizing the shapes displayed. In working to achieve the extrinsic rewards, the children gain considerable practice at a basic skill.

Extrinsic rewards as sources of self-esteem

Put most simply, extrinsic rewards do more than provide information about performance, they can also result in enhancing the user's enjoyment of an activity and pleasure at a good performance which is indicated by the presence of external rewards. Performance of the activity can thus become associated with personal satisfaction derived from receipt of the reward. In such situations, it is possible to envisage circumstances where the performance of the activity acquires a motivational quality because of its previous associations. The performance has then acquired intrinsically motivating qualities, i.e., the learner will engage in the task for the pleasure of doing so, not for the pleasure to be derived from external rewards. Note that in such a situation, external manipulations have resulted in the development of intrinsic motivation.

There thus appears to be a dilemma. The use of external rewards as supported by operant conditioning theory does not adequately deal with situations where intrinsic motivation decreases as a consequence of the use of external rewards. However, use of external rewards is widely used with apparently satisfactory motivational consequences. The resolution to this apparent conflict lies in the way in which the external reward is perceived and cognitively evaluated by the learner.

Cognitive evaluation and intrinsic motivation

Following performance of an activity both extrinsic and intrinsic outcomes occur. The extrinsic outcomes result from environmental controls and circumstances and include the types of external rewards mentioned above. The intrinsic outcomes result from the learner's emotions and evaluations in response to the performance, the extrinsic consequences and the relationships between them. In such a framework, there is not a simple relationship between the provision of an external reward and the probability of a particular performance. Contributing to the likelihood of the learner repeating the behaviour is the way in which the learner evaluates the behaviour and its consequences. If the learner places an importance on the external consequences (external rewards) then the behaviour is likely to be repeated and intrinsic motivation maintained or enhanced. If little value or importance is attached, then intrinsic motivation will decline and the use of external rewards be of little consequence. This view of intrinsic motivation (derived from Deci, 1975 and Keller, 1983) helps explain the apparent dilemma referred to above. Deci utilises three propositions in support of cognitive evaluation:

1. Intrinsic motivation decreases as the perceived locus of causality shifts from internal to external.
2. A reduction in intrinsic motivation will result if the learner's feelings of competence, efficacy and self-determination are reduced; conversely, intrinsic motivation will be enhanced if the above feelings are increased.
3. Every reward has two elements – a controlling element and an informational element. If the controlling element is dominant, this will shift the perceived locus of causality to an external agent reducing intrinsic motivation. If the informational element is dominant, it will enhance feelings of competence and self-determination, i.e., being in control.

In considering operant conditioning theory, it was mentioned that use of extrinsic rewards could sometimes reduce intrinsic motivation and, at other times, apparently increase it. The resolution lies in the extent to which the use of an external reinforcer is viewed by the learner as having a controlling influence. A reward which is usually associated with a task is *not* perceived as having a controlling influence. Thus, traditional classroom rewards can be seen as customarily following on from good performance – they are associated with the task, and are perceived as such by the children. In such situations, we would not anticipate any reduction in intrinsic motivation. What this implies is that extrinsic rewards are appropriate when they can be associated with the task. Broadly speaking, we can perhaps summarise the role of cognitive evaluation by stating that intrinsic motivation can be supported by the use of external rewards when those rewards have a significance and a value to the child and when their receipt contributes to the child's feelings of competence and efficacy. The ensuing interaction between the extrinsic and intrinsic consequences is likely to contribute positively to intrinsic motivation, influencing the child's desire to carry on or repeat the activity.

Motivational software and motivational theories

The relationships between extrinsic and intrinsic motivation are clearly not simple. However, if we are to attain a deeper level of understanding of the motivational qualities of computer games, it is important that we go beyond explanations that emphasize the 'bells and whistles' or novelty value of the technology. Although these are undoubtedly influential, such variables as impressive sound or graphic effects are likely to be short lasting. Unfortunately, in some instances the use of the technology to attract attention in this manner has been assumed to be its main motivational quality. The amount of work which has been carried out in the field of motivation is considerable, but relatively little of this work has influenced educational practice. An attention-gaining strategy which works today might not work tomorrow because its novelty value is lost. Although novelty and dramatic effects can be used to gain attention, it is unsatisfactory to assume that these must always be present in order to promote efficient learning and to maintain motivation. What is required is an analysis which brings together the more enduring features of learners and of materials that appear to contribute to sustained motivation.

Of the factors identified by Malone's analyses, three stand out as being particularly significant – challenge, fantasy and curiosity, each of which can be related to psychological perspectives on motivation.

Challenge

The presence of challenge is demonstrated by the existence of variable levels of difficulty together with the presence of clearly defined goals. These are common features of many computer games. The game environment sets the player a series of challenges to overcome. These are often graded in difficulty so that the player moves through a series of levels. Within each level of difficulty challenges also exist and two significant components to challenge are particularly significant:

1. *Personal relevance* The challenges should be personally meaningful, accessible and feedback should be provided about performance. Thus, the player should be able to relate to the nature of the challenge. This does not mean that the game environment should be within the realm of the child's direct everyday experiences, but that the game environment should be one that the child wants to enter, i.e., that there is some initial motivation to become involved with the game. Further, the problems or challenges presented should be within the player's initial competence, so that the child feels that success is likely. If the problems are too complex, then a loss of interest is likely to occur as feelings of failure develop. Cognitively, the provision of 'accessible' problems implies that the player can activate relevant schemata. The provision of challenge results in disequilibrium, and success results in accommodation and in the development of feelings of competence and efficacy. The provision of feedback concerning performance can assist the player as it indicates whether progress is being made, again contributing to a feeling of self-competence as a successful resolution of the goal is approached. For this reason, many games inform the player of the criterion levels required to progress to the next level. Informing the learner of the objective in this manner sets a cognitive expectancy. The satisfaction of this expectancy can be intrinsically motivating.

2. *Uncertain outcome*   The provision of variable levels of difficulty and hidden information falls into this category. Well-designed games enable a player to enter at a relatively low skill level, but as expertise grows, the player moves on to more difficult levels. These often require the exercise of a new skill in addition to those skills utilized at an earlier level. Often the new skill may be little more than 'expert' performance of an old skill (e.g., faster reaction times). However, some games demand the utilization of additional skills, often requiring the monitoring of several information sources together with decision making and additional motor skills. In such contexts, well-designed games can be seen as presenting a hierarchical situation in which the player moves towards a final end point through mastering a series of skills which move from simple to complex or from novice to expert. Within such a hierarchy, new information and new challenges (not known at the outset, hence uncertain) can be introduced at each level.

Fantasy

The provision of a fantasy environment is a common feature of many computer games. Fantasy can be defined as 'imagination unrestricted by reality' (*Collins Concise English Dictionary*), and it plays a common role in everyday life in the form of books, films, board games, day dreaming, social activities and TV and radio programmes, so it is not surprising that game designers have incorporated a strong fantasy element into games. Two aspects of fantasy can be identified:

1. *Extrinsic*   Here the fantasy depends on the use of the skills and the problems presented are independent of any fantasy element. So for example, in the game 'Hangman' the exercise of the skill does not depend in any way on the fantasy – the same fantasy could be used in a variety of problems. A similar example applies where the child has to perform simple calculations, identify shapes, spell words correctly in order to secure the 'reward' of shooting down imaginary invaders.
2. *Intrinsic*   In intrinsic fantasies, the fantasy depends on the skill and the skill on the fantasy. The problems are presented as an integral part of the fantasy element. Thus, a fantasy

environment can be created which presents challenges embedded within the fantasy theme. Successful resolution of the problems requires the exercise of particular skills. The important thing about intrinsic fantasy is that the exercise of the skill is an integral part of the game situation. Thus, in an adventure game format, the child may explore an imaginary environment, exercising reading, communication and problem-solving skills. These are an essential component of the fantasy environment and without the exercise of the skills, the exploration could not continue.

Malone found that games making use of intrinsic fantasy were more satisfying and motivating than those using extrinsic fantasy. One reason for this is that with intrinsic fantasy the resolution of the fantasy is intimately linked to the nature of the fantasy. If the fantasy environment is one that the child has decided to enter, then the solution of the challenges becomes of considerable personal significance, as they are part of the fantasy world.

In general, the use of fantasy environments (simulations and adventure games are obvious examples) can help the learner utilize existing knowledge in situations other than those usually encountered in the classroom. For many children, it might be more motivating to have to work out how far a spaceship has to travel to a particular planet to pick up supplies, fuel and passengers than to have to calculate the length of the hypotenuse on a triangle. The skills required may be the same, but the context in which they are expressed may be very different. It is this aspect which makes the fantasy motivating, and which may also provide a more accurate assessment of existing abilities. Sylvia Weir (1987) provides another example which illustrates this point that performance can sometimes depend on context. One of the cerebral palsied subjects she worked with demonstrated great difficulty in manipulating the screen turtle to a target on the screen using simple commands. However, when the task was re-designed in such a way that the subject suggested her own fantasy scenarios performance improved dramatically. It would thus appear that the use of fantasy environments is not only motivating, but can also tap unexpressed cognitive skills.

Curiosity

The third major factor identified by Malone is that of curiosity. This enters both the challenge and fantasy categories summarized above. Cognitive curiosity can be linked to the 'I wonder what will happen if . . .' element of hypothesis testing. However, it is important that the level of curiosity/exploration made possible is at an optimal level for existing skills. Too much uncertainty of outcome may result in a loss of motivation, as may too predictable an outcome. Essentially, the attempt to build 'curiosity' into a program assumes that the user will seek to initiate exploratory activities in order to gain a better understanding or mastery of the environment. It is more than simple 'perceptual or sensory curiosity' which refers mainly to attention-attracting features. Cognitive curiosity relates to the internal processes of cognitive development involving assimilation and accommodation. On this perspective, the way to engage curiosity is to present enough information to make existing understanding incomplete. The resultant cognitive uncertainty (disequilibrium) motivates the individual to resolve the problem leading to the development of a more sophisticated level of understanding (accommodation). Given this, it is important that consideration is given towards the child's existing ability levels and the extent to which these can be developed through the software. Environments which do not enable the child to gain a sense of active cognitive involvement, meaningful feedback (i.e., providing information which can be utilized by the learner) and personal control and influence are unlikely to be intrinsically motivating.

The significance of autonomy

The factors of challenge, fantasy and curiosity can be subsumed under the general heading of autonomy. Intrinsic motivation appears to be enhanced in situations where learners can exercise control in such a way that they feel that mastery of the situation can be attained. In such situations, the users' self-perceptions and self-respect can be enhanced by succeeding at the challenges presented or by seeing that progress is being made (via the appropriate use of feedback). Many learners (particularly impaired students) have been placed in situations where they are essentially passive, i.e., the situation controls them. Malone's analyses, together with the earlier discussion of motivation, indicate that internal motivation can be increased by the provision of the opportunity to exercise control and autonomy in a personally significant and challenging environment.

It is significant that amongst the advantages cited for the use of the language Logo is its potential to provide the opportunity for learner control in the context of solving personal challenges. The underlying rationale here is essentially one which is based on giving the user a tool for control and communication, and can be seen as having a close relationship to many ideas within psychology. Thus, both Piaget and Bruner spoke of constructivism, i.e., the view that children actively construct their own knowledge through interactions with the surrounding environment. More specifically, Deci (1975) refers to intrinsic motivation being closely related to the learner being in control, and the cognitive scientists Bereiter and Scardamelia (1983) talk of children 'taking charge of their own minds' within an intentional learning framework. The model essentially states that internal motivation comes from a feeling of autonomy or control, and that, consequently, intrinsic motivation will be enhanced by activities which enable children to exercise such autonomy. Within this there is:

1. *A will for mastery*　　Psychological theory states that humans have 'drives' which motivate them to seek mastery of new situations which are slightly more complex than those already mastered.
2. *Hypothesis testing*　　In order to gain mastery/understanding of a situation, humans must form and evaluate hypotheses, i.e., they must explore new situations to see whether their current levels of knowledge and understanding are adequate. Human cognitive growth is seen as stemming from such hypothesis testing.
3. *Assimilation of new data/information to existing schemata*　　If the current level of understanding/ability is sufficient to deal with the new situation, then that information is incorporated into current schemata. However, if the schemata are not

adequate, then modifications have to take place if the new situation is to be mastered.

4. *Accommodation based on a will for mastery* The process of schema modification is closely connected with the 'will for mastery'. New situations which are slightly more complex than can be dealt with by existing schemata cause uncertainty and curiosity – disequilibrium. If, however, the new situation is cognitively accessible (in the sense given above) then the will for mastery results in the learner striving to achieve that mastery and to restore equilibrium. In such a manner, new understanding is developed through the related processes of assimilation and accommodation.

In practical terms what this implies is that learning environments should contain sufficient complexity to enable assimilation and accommodation to take place. The learner should be able to utilize present knowledge and understanding, but should also be presented with new problem situations which are accessible to those levels of knowledge and understanding. These problem situations should act to stimulate curiosity as a result of the challenges presented, but should also provide the learner with a feeling of autonomy.

In such an interpretation, it is clear that the design of the learning environments is of paramount importance in determining whether they will be intrinsically motivating. A major feature implied both by theoretical considerations and by research evidence is the role of challenge within the environments. Challenge is important because it establishes the complexity of the environment (and hence its accessibility) and also provides the potential for user autonomy as a result of successful mastery of the challenges presented.

Autonomy, self-esteem and locus of control

As indicated above, several theoretical frameworks can be related to the work on motivational variables, with three broad classes of theory being relevant. One group of theorists relates intrinsic motivation to the concepts of challenge, mastery and self-competence. Such models emphasize humans as problem solvers, and intrinsic motivation is perceived as stemming from individuals' attempts to solve problems and accomplish goals that require the use of personally salient skills. What this means for the design of instructional activities is that they should incorporate a sequence of goals which are within the competence of the target users. This would also seem to imply that the tasks should be hierarchically structured so that new goals and challenges are presented as the learner acquires mastery. In this formulation, an important component is the sense of personal achievement which results from success.

Although the role of challenge, goal setting and the view of humans as problem solvers presents an important framework for the development of personally motivating educational environments, it tends to overlook one important dimension, that of the personality of the user. If the learning environment is designed to present challenges and to set goals, then the implicit assumption is that the learners will respond positively to the presence of such challenges, i.e., will be intrinsically motivated. Cronbach and Snow (1977), however, have distinguished between two kinds of motivational variables. 'Defensive motivation' refers to the level of anxiety as shown in the learner's reaction to perceived 'threats' (challenges), and 'constructive motivation' refers to the learner's wish to achieve success when faced by challenge. The anxiety felt by an individual may well influence performance when dealing with challenge.

Research on the effects of anxiety on performance have indicated that some students are more strongly motivated by fear of failure than others. They may respond to challenging situations in inefficient ways and may seek to avoid challenges, thereby not fitting the hypothesized view of humans as internally motivated problem solvers. Other students show lower levels of anxiety when faced by challenge; do not fear failure; are not worried about the possibility of making errors, and work hard to overcome difficulties and achieve the goals established.

What this implies is that we should be cautious about assuming that the presence of goals and challenges in software will motivate *all* students in the same way. They may motivate some, but others may respond by seeking to avoid the situation. This may then have further consequences for perceived self-efficacy and competence, adversely influencing future motivation. An important component here appears to be that of the student's own perception of his/her ability when faced by challenge. The concept of 'locus of control' refers to a learner's expectancy concerning the controlling influences on reinforcements. A learner who assumes that good performance is a consequence of personal effort can be regarded as an internally orientated person. In contrast, an externally orientated individual tends to attribute consequences to external circumstances.

Locus of control

Weiner (1978) has utilized the concept of locus of control into 'attribution theory' and has argued that the way students approach challenge may influence their interpretation of success and failure. Those students who tackle challenges positively will tend to attribute success to their own efforts and abilities. For such students, failure or difficulty is likely to be attributed to lack of effort, with the response being increased persistence and determination. In contrast, students who display high anxiety concerning new situations and new challenges are more likely to attribute failure to external variables (not lack of effort) and to respond by giving up. The consequences for perceived self-competence are that those students who attribute success to ability and failure to lack of effort will tend to possess higher self-concepts than those attributing failure to factors perceived as being outside their control. In a similar context is the distinction deCharms (1976) draws between 'origins' and 'pawns'. Origins tend to be active authors of their own behaviour, whereas pawns are more reactive and let their goals and habits be dictated by others. deCharms argues that educational activities need to be designed to develop a higher degree of origin behaviour. A final concept relevant to this discussion of students' attitudes towards challenge is that of 'learned helplessness' (Seligman, 1975). Learned helplessness develops when a child wants to succeed but cannot avoid a situation in which success is expected but is not possible. In such situations, failure is inevitable, and the child comes to associate failure with particular activities. Once established, learned helplessness is difficult to reverse.

Expectancy

In general, the use of challenges is predicted by the view that humans are motivated by a will to achieve mastery in problem situations. This has resulted in the development of educational environments designed to present challenge. Within such a paradigm there is also an implicit assumption that learners will have a personal expectancy for success. However, personal expectancy for success (positive self-efficacy) is influenced by past experience with success or failure at the given task, perceived locus of control (internal or external) and personal causation. Learners who possess a history of failure and/or difficulty on a particular task and who attribute performance on that task to external factors are not likely to be motivated by environments which present challenges within that task domain. Where such a possibility occurs it emphasizes the importance of considering the learners' cognitive expectancy concerning the activity. Where expectancies are low, strategies need to be adopted which lead to a shift towards higher expectancy for success when faced by challenge. Keller (1983) suggests a number of strategies, including:

1. Increase the expectancy for success by increasing experience with success in similar situations.
2. Increase expectancy for success by using techniques which allow for personal control of success.
3. Increase expectancy for success by using feedback which enables students to establish a link between their own efforts and good performance (success).

Well-designed educational environments can take all these factors into account and incorporate the positive role of challenge. However, it would be naïve to assume that the simple presence of challenge will of itself be intrinsically motivating. It has to be placed in a context of personal expectancy. Rubincam and Olivier (1985) of the Ontario Institute for Studies in Education report a finding of relevance here. On a program designed to evaluate mathematical skills, students were given a choice between going straight to a test exercise or going through a series of practice items. Rubincam and Olivier found a divergence of choices with some students going straight to the test and others opting for the longer route via the practice items. One interpretation of this is that the former group had higher confidence in their own abilities (positive expectancy and efficacy) than did the latter group.

What such considerations seem to imply is that the use of challenge should be exercised cautiously. It can be an important factor in influencing intrinsic motivation, but not all students will respond to the presence of challenge in the same way. Where expectancies of success are high, challenges will be motivating. Where they are low, the presence of challenges which do not take expectancy into account is likely to result in a loss of motivation. What is implied is the design and application of software which takes into account such individual differences in expectancy, possibly offering different routes to established goals. Alternative routes could incorporate some of Keller's strategies for increasing positive expectancy in order to influence cognitive evaluation of outcomes so that enhanced motivation ensues.

Autonomy and self control

The link between intrinsic motivation and perceived control and self-determination is one emphasized by a second, related group of theories. Here, the interpretation is not one that sees intrinsic motivation as originating in successful problem solving, but rather that humans are regarded as active agents seeking to exert control and influence over their environments. In this model, intrinsically motivating activities are those which provide the opportunity to exercise control, and motivation originates with such control, rather than with problem solving *per se*.

Paul Goldenberg (1979) has identified individual self-competence in computer-mediated situations as originating in the learner's ability to exercise control over the computer environment. The potential of Logo to be used in this manner accounts for Goldenberg's enthusiasm for its use with special-needs children (physically handicapped, cognitively impaired, etc.). Often, such children have been unable to exercise active control over their immediate environment because of the nature of the impairment. Researchers like Goldenberg and Sylvia Weir attest to the potential of Logo to enable such control to be exercised, often resulting in dramatic reassessment of individual abilities and potential.

Within this context, it is easy to see why use of Logo has generated such enthusiasm. The ease of use of turtle graphics encourages active manipulation of the screen or floor turtle. For physically impaired children, such manipulation is made possible via the use of simple control mechanisms, often enabling the child to demonstrate previously unappreciated abilities. In a sense, the structure of the Logo language encourages such individual freedom of action and control over the environment.

Limitations of user freedom

As appealing as this is, the reality is that excessive freedom within a software environment may not result in increased intrinsic motivation. Extreme open-endedness and user freedom can be seen as possible shortcomings as students may experience a lack of purpose with resulting confusion concerning objectives. Given that Malone's analyses have indicated the importance of the presence of goals, it would appear that even where considerable freedom of action is made available, there is a need for goals to be established, either by the teacher, the program or the learner. The provision of goals provides a purpose and a framework within which the learner can operate. There thus appears to be a dilemma. The establishment of goals and challenges may not be appropriate for all learners because of individual differences in responsiveness to challenges and perceived threats. However, the removal of goals may result in a lack of progress in the absence of any set criteria of performance. One possible solution is the provision of hierarchical challenges where students can have the option to move immediately to greater levels of difficulty or can progress through a sequence of activities which move closer to the desired end point. A further alternative is to encourage the students to establish their own goals, rather than having the goals imposed from without. In such a situation – self-imposed goals – the spirit of perceived personal freedom is retained within a context of established goals and challenges appropriate to the skills and potential of individual learners.

Difficulties with goals

The concept of self-imposed goals is not without its problems. In seeking to retain freedom of action and autonomy, thereby enabling the learner to feel in control of the situation, a possibility is that the learner will set inappropriate goals. These may be too easy so that progress does not occur, or may be too difficult so that frustration, disappointment and loss of motivation result with adverse effects on expectancy. Such possibilities imply that considerable attention must be paid to the design of the computer-based learning environments within which learners will exercise freedom. Such environments should offer the possibility of user autonomy but within the restrictions of a defined and structured set of possibilities.

Two examples will illustrate what is involved here. The use of Logo has provided several illustrations of the 'conflict' between user freedom and loss of 'direction'. The Israeli researcher, Uri Leron (1985) has reported that with high school students familiar with Logo there is a need to impose a degree of structure in order to reduce confusion and to enable user-initiated exploration to occur. Working with younger children in Canada, Cohen and Geva (1986) have also emphasised the importance of simplified Logo environments where only a small number of commands can be used. Such environments, they maintain, reduce the difficulty young children experience in learning Logo, but retain the exploratory possibilities in that the children are free to use the simplified and restricted commands in any way they choose. Leron argues that

From an educational point of view, a good study guide seems paradoxically to enhance students' autonomy rather than suppress it. Properly used, it becomes part of the environment with which they interact, giving them more power to achieve their goals without help from the teacher.

Leron's conclusion is an important one, based as it is, on considerable experience of Logo in use in the classroom. However, the basic theoretical underpinning remains, i.e., that students will be more motivated in situations where they can exert control over their own learning. Increased motivation will be indicated by such factors as increased cognitive commitment, longer attention spans, deeper levels of processing and more time on task.

Self-monitoring of learning

Within this model, at least as it is applied to educational technology, is an embedded assumption that learners can exercise this control in such a way so as to determine their own learning. This is a considerable responsibility to place upon young or naïve learners, as it requires that the learners monitor their own progress, whilst simultaneously acquiring new skills and abilities – in other words, that learners reflect upon their own thinking, in order to relate it to their goals and to present performance. In surveying some of the literature on such learner control, Carrier (1984) reports that young and/or naïve learners do not necessarily make good judgements. They select problems which are too easy or too difficult; they select modes of presentation which lead to lower achievement, and they end instruction too early. Carrier concludes that

. . . the less familiar students are with the content, the greater their need for clearly stated objectives, explicit highlighting of important points, requirements for overt responding, and other guidance devices.

If learners are to exercise such control (take control of their own minds) then they must utilize a number of general purpose cognitive skills – decision making, planning, evaluation, self-regulation and reflection on new understandings and misconceptions. Such metacognitive skills are not characteristically possessed by young learners. There is, however, a growing body of evidence which indicates that young learners can be trained in the use of metacognitive skills, and that their utilization results in positive academic gains. The goal for designers of learning environments which promote learner control is thus one of establishing environments which enable the learner to establish goals, monitor on-going learning, and which provide support when and where required.

Autonomous goals

The work of Lawler (1982, 1985) is relevant here. Lawler established computer environments which enabled his young daughter to create scenes related to her everyday experience.

One of the best known of these is the 'Beach' microworld. Lawler discussed with his daughter the things that could be found by the sea. He then created these as Logo procedures (e.g., boat, man, fish, sun, sand, sea) and provided her with a set of cards which showed the names of the procedures. On typing in a word (e.g., sun), a picture of a sun appeared on the screen. In this way it was possible to create a number of pictures showing different beach scenes. Lawler reports that the use of such an approach was both highly motivating and assisted his daughter to develop early reading skills. The important point to consider here is that the environment created was a restricted one, but that it allowed considerable freedom of action to create any scene desired from the words available. The decision as to which words to use, and hence what type of picture to produce was left to the child. She was thus exercising decision-making and goal-setting behaviour, i.e., the initiatives came from her, not from the program.

This ability to set autonomous goals is not restricted to cognitively able children. The Educational Technology Research Group at the University of Hull in England has developed a program which allows severely cognitively impaired children to decide which of 12 pictures they would like to create. Having decided on a picture, this is then displayed on one half of the screen. Each picture is composed of simple geometric shapes, and the child builds up a matching image by selecting the appropriate shapes on a touch-sensitive keyboard. Guidance is provided by the outline of the target shape flashing within the whole picture. A development of this program allows pupils to use pre-defined shapes to produce on-screen pictures. This can lead to further extensions where these pictures are presented as challenges to other pupils.

As in the 'Beach' environment, this software presents a limited set of options, but initiative and goal setting is left to the learner. Again the learner establishes the goal, but within a defined context. In the Hull program, successful accomplishment of the task requires the use of a range of skills including shape discrimination, shape constancy and simple mental rotation activities – recognizing that a triangle remains a triangle whatever its size and orientation. Many learning-impaired children traditionally experience problems with such activities, and observations of the program in use indicate that not only can children succeed in these activities but that they find the task more motivating when they are able to establish their own goals than when an adult suggests which picture to create.

Such environments maintain the spirit of autonomy and control, but can also embody important educational activities and concepts. They provide computer-based microworlds which contain important ideas and principles for the user to learn. These 'important ideas' are analogous to Papert's 'powerful ideas' which are basically skills valued by society. Papert emphasizes the use of Logo programming activities to promote mathematical skills, procedural thinking and problem solving. The important feature here is not that these have been emphasized in the context of Logo, but that they fall into a paradigm which emphasizes the importance of user autonomy within the limits of a defined environment. The effectiveness of such microworlds depends on how the computer-mediated learning experiences are structured – on how the microworlds are designed, the nature of the interactions they permit, the powerful ideas they incorporate and the feedback they provide. Lawler has referred to this design process as 'cognitive engineering' and alludes to the designers of computer learning experiences as 'architects of inner space'.

The role of curiosity

The concept of environments which promote exploration and discovery raises the third general class of theories related to intrinsic motivation. So far, the discussion has concentrated upon explanations of intrinsic motivation in terms of either challenge/goal setting or in terms of perceived control and autonomy. A third general approach focuses on such concepts as curiosity, complexity or discrepancy. This paradigm emphasizes the role of humans as processors of information, deriving satisfaction from activities which provide an optimal level of surprise or complexity in relation to initial skills. The optimal level is normally seen as one which is at an intermediate point – neither too simple nor too complex. The problem is, of course, determining what that intermediate level is as each student may bring different levels of competence to the learning situation.

The general concept of curiosity is embedded within the 'microworlds' framework outlined above and is embodied by the conjectural style of software. Students are seen as being intrinsically motivated by environments which promote a sense of curiosity; a 'What will happen next?' or 'I wonder what will happen if I try . . .?'. Environments will only be satisfying to the extent that they respond to such exploration. This is closely related to the role of 'interesting things' happening within microworlds. The 'interesting things' should be interesting to the learner, which again presents problems as not only do students bring different levels of competence, but also they bring different interests. This implies that, if possible, the 'interesting things' should be defined by the learner, i.e., learners should have some control over the activities. Logo and other programming activities are essentially of this nature. Again, however, the interpretation is that although curiosity can be built into a program, important aspects relate to individual differences and the extent to which autonomy can be exercised and challenges established.

Environments which are designed to contain features which will stimulate curiosity, uncertainty, and which are at an intermediate level of discrepancy can be related to the Piagetian concepts of equilibrium, assimilation and accommodation. The uncertainty results in disequilibrium, as the learner seeks to assimilate the data into existing schemata. Modification of the relevant schemata occurs by accommodation returning the learner to a state of equilibrium. Further incongruity and uncertainty again results in disequilibrium with resultant accommodation. The implicit assumption is that the learner will gain a greater understanding as a result of the design of environments which create uncertainty, incongruity and complexity. There is also the further assumption that humans are internally driven to resolve such uncertainties.

Overview

These three theoretical frameworks – humans as problem solvers, humans as information processors, and humans as organisms seeking to exercise control and self-determination –

are not incompatible, nor necessarily distinct. Indeed, many apparently motivating computer environments contain aspects of all three approaches. They are challenging, they allow for user freedom and they contain surprise and incongruity. What is not clear is the extent to which any of these three approaches can act independently of the others. The use of microcomputers in education may enable us to specify more clearly the relative contribution of these approaches in influencing intrinsic motivation. Such research would not only benefit the design of learning environments generally, but would also enhance the level of theoretical formulation, as the need to incorporate a theoretical model in the design stages would shift the emphasis of the theories from being essentially descriptive to being prescriptive.

Problems

Although this might appear to be a relatively straightforward process, it contains a number of complexities. If, for example, we consider the role of challenge to be a major influence on extrinsic motivation, and the evidence would lead one to such a conclusion, then some of the problems become apparent. Mention has already been made of the fact that students may differ in their reactions to challenges, and that, for some, the setting of goals within software may not be motivating, because of low expectancy of success. Although there are possible solutions to this, for example, the provision of the opportunity to move gradually through practice items to reduce the perceived 'threat', the reality is that we do not yet have the research evidence which would tell us if this is likely to be a successful strategy.

In addition, the possibility of enabling learners to establish their own goals is also problematic because it requires sophisticated self-monitoring of performance, and there is little research evidence to support the notion that total student control results in more effective learning. For these reasons, the concept of microworlds was implied as a possible resolution of some of the problems. Although this seems to be a move in the right direction, problems remain. Invariably, within microworlds there exists a set of possibilities. The microworlds have the potential to enhance levels of understanding via the process of exploration. However, there is no guarantee that the potential present will actually be utilized by the learner. This again takes us back to the possibility of imposed goals and structure, albeit within an exploratory framework. However, the exploration now implied is much more of a directed or guided exploration. As learners master one concept or level of difficulty, they move on to the next level, so that theoretically an optimal level of challenge/difficulty or incongruity is present.

So far, in theory, so good – exploration and the perception of autonomy is retained; challenge is present, as are incongruity or curiosity. Many current educational and game programs do, in fact, incorporate such elements, so that as learners attain a particular level of performance they move automatically on to the next level of difficulty. There is, however, a potential flaw in many such programs, which is that the learner may not be aware of the imposed hierarchy, nor is there a provision to review progress. Just as the learner feels that mastery is *being* acquired, the program automatically decides that mastery *has been* attained and presents new, more complex material. An important feature in learning is the self-confidence which develops as a result of knowing that you can perform a certain activity or demonstrate a set of skills. Materials which continually leave the learner in a state of uncertainty because of presenting increasingly difficult challenges may result in a loss of motivation rather than increase motivation.

Review what is known

Gagne and Briggs (1979) refer to the importance of reviewing material already covered and activating relevant previous knowledge in preparing to tackle new activities. Both of these can be seen as relevant here, not from the perspective of instructional design (Gagne and Briggs' major area of contribution) but from a cognitive viewpoint. Reviewing material enables learners to evaluate their own performance, and activating prior knowledge can be seen as a form of 'cognitive warm up' in preparation for new tasks. The emphasis here, however, is upon how the learner perceives and interprets the situation. In a sense, in reviewing material, going over past activities, the learner is forming a hypothesis. The hypothesis is 'I believe I can do this, but I will just check', and this is tested by review or practice. If the hypothesis is confirmed then satisfaction is derived. In Gagne's terms, we set a cognitive expectancy by such a form of hypothesis testing where we inform ourselves of what the objective is. Reinforcement comes from confirming that expectancy. Many parents would attest to the motivational qualities present in confirming young children's expectancies. If, for example, we consider the commonplace activity of reading a story to young children, many would confirm the fact that the same story may be requested on many occasions. Numerous games and social interactions can result from such activities (missing out words, putting in the wrong words, etc.), but one interpretation is that in requesting the same story, children derive pleasure initially from confirming their expectancies of what will happen in the story. Equally, how often as adults do we play a favourite piece of music? One source of pleasure comes from the confirmation of the expectancies established. We should seek to design learning environments which do not just encourage hypothesis testing and exploration, but we should also be aware that hypothesis testing does not just apply to unknown situations. It also applies to what we think we know, and can be a source of confidence and enhanced self-esteem.

Motivation can thus come from incorporating the option for review or for practice on activities that have already been acquired. The important aspect here is the user's perception of performance, not the program's perception. Internal motivation comes from the extent to which the learner feels that mastery has been attained. Continuous challenge may not allow for the development of positive expectancies. If learners invariably feel they are struggling, this is likely to result in a loss of motivation. Children have a right to find something challenging so that accommodation can take place. They also have the right to develop their self-image by demonstrating their competence at things they can do.

Conclusion

The issue of the motivational qualities of educational software is therefore one which contains a number of inter-relating factors. In practice, little experimental work has been carried out to examine the issues raised. Malone initiated research in this field and provided a framework for analysing a number of issues, an aspect developed in more detail by Malone and Lepper (1983). Lepper (1985) has also drawn attention to the fact that although we have a body of evidence and theory relating motivation to software, we know very little about how motivation actually affects learning. Malone's original research question was what made software appealing (i.e., enjoyable) *not* how these factors influenced performance. Lepper has suggested four further areas worthy of additional experimental investigation:

1. The relationships between differing motivational variables and attention spans.
2. Whether differing motivational variables promote differences in involvement with the activity.
3. Whether variations in motivational appeal result in variations in 'arousal'.
4. Whether the addition of motivational features provides a useful means of representing abstract problems.

Underlying these questions is the central issue of whether educational activities that are 'enjoyable' or 'fun' promote more effective learning. The assumption is that they do, but this remains very much an open question. If they do, it is possible that they do so via the fact that children are likely to spend longer on activities they find enjoyable, and that any improvements in performance would be due to the general variable of 'time on task', rather than being intrinsic to some motivational feature which enhanced the degree of cognitive engagement. Lepper points out that the incorporation of motivational variables into the design of educational software provides us with a research opportunity to examine the interactions between these variables and learning. The necessity of specifying precisely the nature of those variables in programmable terms should result in advances in the formulation of the underlying theories. More significantly, microcomputers provide us with the opportunity to manipulate the variables under well-defined conditions. This gives the potential for examining more closely what are the most effective motivational features and may result in both the design of more effective learning environments and the development of better models.

6 *Logo*

A Link between Theory and Practice?

Logo, with its turtle graphics, has blazed a trail through the undergrowth of microworld creation and left behind it a body of literature laying out the potentialities of the system. It has created a vision in which the only true god is Logo and his chief disciple is Papert. As with all revelatory religions, the euphoria of the early period of conversion and proselytising has given way to an air of scepticism, with a rising level of incredulity and disbelief.
(Nichol, 1988)

Logo has the potential to be one of the most important of the computer-based intellectual tools for education.
(Bork, 1985)

It seems that Papert's vision of radical educational advance by a process of self-discovery learning using LOGO is, in truth, little short of 'technoromanticism'. All the available evidence seems to suggest that the method of learning he advocates will be, at best, unspectacular and, at worst, haphazard and unreliable.
(Simon, 1987)

Logo: the culture

Of all the various approaches to computer-based education, the influence of Logo and of one of its designers, Seymour Papert, stand out as being of perhaps the most importance. In terms of citations in the literature on computer applications in education, Papert is the most referred-to author, gathering twice as many citations as any other contributor in the field (Rubincam, 1987). It is safe to assume that any reference to Papert will invariably

119

contain a reference to Logo, and that the combination of Papert and Logo represents the most influential work in this field. References to Papert and Logo are not restricted to a specific issue but tend to address a variety of themes. Thus, some authors cite Papert as a major influence in the general context of computer applications; others describe the nature of the Logo language; others concentrate on evaluation of the claims made for the use of Logo, whereas other writers have addressed theoretical and pedagogical issues raised by Papert's advocacy of the use of Logo in schools. Thus, any discussion of computer-assisted learning cannot ignore the issues raised by Logo, nor can any evaluation of Logo examine its influence in isolation of a variety of wider educational considerations.

In many senses, one of Papert's major contributions has been to direct attention to a wide range of issues which can be raised in the broad context of computer-mediated education, but for which Logo seems to act as an exemplar. There are several reasons why this should be. In the first instance, the approach advocated by Papert is one of the few which claims a dominant psychological rationale. Papert has a view of children as builders of their own intellectual structures, a perspective profoundly influenced by Piagetian psychology. Where Papert departs from Piaget is in the importance he attributes to the culture which surrounds the growing child. In Papert's perspective, the culture provides the materials for cognitive growth. Where such materials are provided in abundance, then intellectual growth is facilitated. Papert's basic position is that intellectual development can be accelerated given the appropriate environmental stimuli. For Papert, the potential contribution of the computer lies in extending the range of materials or experiences which will help children build their own intellectual structures. Thus, the computer becomes an intellectual tool or an 'object to think with'.

Papert's influence, however, goes beyond this. Like Piaget, he views learning as a constructive process in which optimum understanding comes when children build their own mental models. In order to achieve this, Papert advocates an active role for the child (the child in control of the computer), with learners being in control and responsible for their own learning. Inevitably, this has been associated with a child-centred discovery approach to learning in which children discover knowledge for themselves in ways suited to their own individual learning styles. For Papert, the likely consequences of such an approach are significant. Not only will children gain greater insights into the subject matter they are studying, but, most significantly, they will gain greater insights into the nature of their own thinking and problem-solving strategies. Papert's emphasis is thus not a technological one but a cognitive one. For him, the computer is a tool to be used by the learner. His major interest is in 'universal issues of how people think and how they learn to think'. It is about the role computers might play in enhancing the quality of children's thinking, and, in particular, the contribution Logo might make. His advocacy of Logo reflects an approach very different from that encapsulated by more traditional domains of computer-assisted learning. Drawing on notions of liberal education, Papert stresses the need for the computer to provide a set of computational tools which can provide the means by which children can explore, investigate, experiment and, most significantly, construct their own understanding, rather than be the passive recipient of another's understanding.

Papert's themes

We thus have at least three major themes running through Papert's influence. There is a strong psychological component, drawing on Piagetian constructivist philosophy and on information processing theory, but which also addresses the question of the inter-relationships between culture and cognitive development. There is also a pedagogical theme which raises questions concerning not just the best ways to use computers in the classroom, but more fundamental issues of how children learn and the optimum manner to foster learning in a classroom environment. Finally, there are the claims made for the use of Logo. Of particular importance are those which maintain that use of Logo in the manner advocated by Papert will result in major gains in generalizable cognitive skills which will transfer to all areas of the curriculum, i.e., that as a result of programming in Logo children will come to reflect on the nature of their own thinking and on themselves as thinkers.

In the LOGO environment . . .. The child, even at pre-school ages, is in control. The child programs the computer. And in teaching the computer how to think, children embark on an exploration about how they themselves think. The experience can be heady. Thinking about thinking turns the child into an epistemologist, an experience not even shared by most adults. (Papert, 1980)

Such is the vision offered by Papert: computer-based environments which will foster creative, self-discovery learning and which will enable the expression and enhancement of a broad range of powerful cognitive abilities. The vehicle to achieve such a vision is the computer language Logo.

Logo: the language

Logo is a programming language which bears some resemblance to another computer language, LISP, which was designed primarily for list processing applications in artificial intelligence. Although full implementations of Logo do possess a list processing facility, the features most frequently associated with Logo are 'turtle graphics' and turtle geometry, and these are the aspects most commonly introduced to young children. The 'turtle' can exist in two distinct forms, either physical or symbolic. It can be a robot, controlled from the computer by commands in the Logo language. Early forms of the turtle were transparent dome-shaped robots, linked to the computer by an 'umbilical cord'. More recent Logo turtles have come to resemble more closely 'real' turtles and some versions have dispensed with the physical linkage to the computer and are controlled by an infra-red beam. In whatever form, the control of the turtle is essentially the same. The more symbolic form of the turtle is that which exists on the computer screen, usually depicted as a small triangle. It is this latter form which is most common as it is integral to the Logo language. The physical turtle is an extra and, unfortunately, is often beyond the financial means of schools. There is little doubt that the presence of a physical turtle adds considerably to the additional motivational qualities of Logo.

Children of all ages are intrigued and excited by the idea of controlling the turtle and getting it to move around the floor. A robot moving around the classroom inevitably has more appeal to younger children than one which moves around a screen. Further, it can be argued that, particularly for young children, the physical turtle should form an integral component of the methodology of introduction to Logo.

The essence of the turtle graphics component of Logo is that the user is in control of the turtle (floor or screen). This control is achieved by the use of simple commands like 'FORWARD', 'BACK', 'RIGHT', 'LEFT', 'PENUP', 'PENDOWN'. In order to control the turtle the user gives a command together with a number and that command is exercised. Thus, 'FORWARD 100' would send the turtle forward by 100 turtle units. In a similar manner, 'RIGHT 45' would turn the turtle through 45 degrees. Initially, these numbers need have no meaning to the user, but the child can discover their significance by experimentation. Commands like 'PENUP' AND 'PENDOWN' control whether the turtle leaves a trace of its passage.

The significance of these commands is that they have meaning to children, and so they can relate their own experiences to them. Thus, children are used to moving forward, backward and turning through space. Part of their everyday activity will involve drawing and moving a pencil to different parts of their paper, sometimes leaving a trace and sometimes not. In Piagetian terms, Logo commands are 'syntonic' with the child's own body and world knowledge so the child can activate this knowledge when introduced to Logo.

Introducing Logo in the classroom

A typical methodology for the introduction of Logo to young children might involve the following steps. In the first instance, the children could be encouraged to play 'turtle games' in which they play the role of robot or controller, using simple commands to move a friend around the room, avoiding obstacles and reaching a target. A particularly appealing version of this involves the children controlling the movement of the teacher. Once the children start deliberately to manoeuvre the teacher into desks, then it is usually a sign that they have fully understood the basic concepts involved! At this stage, a floor turtle could be introduced, and the children encouraged to control the turtle's movement and to experiment with different commands and numbers in order to see their effects. Once the children have gained confidence with the simple commands, they could be given more explicit tasks, or encouraged to generate such tasks for themselves. The drawing of squares, triangles, houses, simple cars and even schematic turtles are examples of tasks undertaken by 8-year-old children following the introduction of a floor turtle in the manner described. Clearly, the fact that the screen and floor turtles can exist independently or in parallel means that in the absence of a floor turtle, screen-based turtle activities can be used.

Teaching the turtle

Once children have reached the level of understanding which enables them to sequence a series of instructions, then it becomes possible to introduce the idea of teaching the turtle a new command, and to introduce the idea of writing a program. Perhaps the most commonly reported example of this is where the sequence of instructions

```
FORWARD 100
RIGHT 90
FORWARD 100
RIGHT 90
FORWARD 100
RIGHT 90
FORWARD 100
RIGHT 90
```

produces a square. Two aspects come into play here. There is the fact that a pattern exists (i.e., the repetition of FORWARD 100 RIGHT 90). If the child perceives the presence of this pattern or can be guided to do so, then the command REPEAT may be introduced, so that

```
REPEAT 4 [FORWARD 100 RIGHT 90]
```

draws the square without the need to have a lengthy sequence of instructions. More significantly, however, is the fact that this set of instructions can be named and 'taught' to the computer. Thus,

```
TO FRED                or        TO BOX
FORWARD 100                      REPEAT 4 [FORWARD 100 RIGHT 90]
RIGHT 90                         END
FORWARD 100
RIGHT 90
FORWARD 100
RIGHT 90
FORWARD 100
RIGHT 90
END
```

will result in a square being drawn each time the command FRED or BOX is used (the names don't matter). If these are then saved on a disc, they can be loaded and used whenever required.

This idea, the ability to teach the computer, is an important one. It involves creating and storing procedures (comprising Logo commands) to achieve particular objectives. The procedures can be used and combined as required in a personal 'tool kit'. Logo can thus be seen as encompassing a broad educational 'philosophy' which stresses learning by experimentation and discovery and which emphasizes the role of the user's own knowledge in establishing particular objectives. On a broader scale it can be seen as an intellectual tool which has the potential to call upon a wide range of general problem-solving skills. Papert's view was that by using Logo for simple programming projects, children would have to exercise the discipline of expressing their ideas and intentions in a simple, formal language (Logo). The presence of errors would call upon other skills (correcting or debugging) in order to get the programs to behave as intended. Papert saw this combination as a potentially powerful means of encouraging important higher-level abilities such as problem solving, project management and the ability to utilize errors as a guide to making improvements.

For example, if a child wanted to use Logo to draw a rocket, several stages of problem solving can be identified. In the first instance, it is necessary to set the problem, in this case to

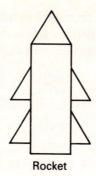

Rocket

Figure 6.1

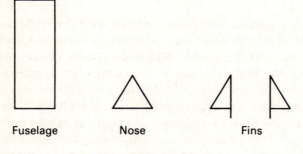

Fuselage   Nose   Fins

Figure 6.2

produce a drawing of a rocket. Having established the objective, it is then necessary to identify the relevant information which will help attain the target (what Logo commands are known and are relevant); to devise a plan; to execute the plan; to evaluate by comparison the product with what is desired, and then to correct if necessary. Several sub-stages can also be identified within this process. If the aim is to produce a rocket (Figure 6.1), a style of procedural thinking can be called on in which both analytical and sequencing skills are utilized. In this style of thinking, said to be encouraged by Logo, the rocket can be analysed into its constituent elements, nose, fuselage and fins, each being simple geometric shapes (Figure 6.2).

Each of these then becomes a sub-problem to be solved, i.e., how to draw each shape. Simple Logo commands can be used in each case:

Shape 1 (fuselage): FD 150 RT 90 FD 50 RT 90 FD 150 RT 90 FD 50 RT 90 END
Shape 2 (nose): RT 30 REPEAT 3 [FD 50 RT 120] LT 30 END
Shape 3 (left fin): FD 50 LT 150 FD 50 LT 120 FD 25 LT 90 END
Shape 4 (right fin): FD 50 RT 150 FD 50 RT 120 FD 25 RT 90 END

Note: FD, RT and LT are Logo abbreviations for Forward, Right and Left respectively. The numbers refer to 'turtle steps' or to degrees of turn, and the REPEAT command instructs the turtle to carry out the actions listed within the brackets the specified number of times.

Having successfully produced the above procedures they can then be combined in a 'super-procedure' called 'Rocket' (these procedures were produced by an 8-year-old). Note that the process of combining procedures introduces additional problem solving. Simply using SHAPE1, SHAPE2, SHAPE3, SHAPE4 will not produce the rocket, it will produce

Figure 6.3

In order to achieve the objective it is necessary to move the turtle to the desired starting points before each procedure is executed. The 'super-procedure' written by the pupil in order to generate the desired picture was: TO ROCKET HOME SHAPE1 FD 150 SHAPE2 BACK 90 SHAPE3 HOME SHAPE3 HOME RT 90 FD 50 LT 90 FD 150 BACK 90 SHAPE4 PU HOME RT 90 FD 50 LT 90 PD SHAPE4 HT. (In this sequence of instructions, the commands PU and PD refer to PENUP and PENDOWN which control whether the turtle leaves a trace of its path. The command HT 'hides' the turtle and HOME sends the turtle to its original starting position.)

This introduces what is perhaps the most significant aspect of Logo as a learning device or 'tool to think with'. It is that in experimenting with commands and in attempting to achieve particular objectives, errors will be made and are to be expected. The visual immediacy of turtle graphics is such that the child can immediately relate what appears on the screen to the desired (imagined) product, and can examine possible reasons why something appears 'to have gone wrong'. Logo falls very much into an educational approach which supports the adage 'we learn from our mistakes'.

Away from turtles

Although Logo is generally associated with its graphics capability, it also contains a powerful list-processing facility for manipulating text. This, however, is considerably less user friendly than turtle graphics, and consequently is less frequently utilized. Mike Sharples, however, of the Cognitive Science Group at the University of Sussex, has reported an approach utilizing Logo's list-processing facility in a manner which can be said to be in accordance with the turtle graphics approach. Sharples (1985) points out that attempts to teach list processing to children and adults have been generally unsuccessful. Individuals who had enjoyed turtle graphics were 'bored and confused by lists.' Sharples' suggestion is that in order to appreciate the potential of list processing as a tool for text manipulation, it is necessary to provide a toolkit which goes beyond the Logo commands for handling lists. Sharples describes two Logo programs which make use of Logo's list-processing capabilities, but which respond to simple commands and which can be used by children.

The first program described by Sharples is 'Phrasebook', which is a direct analogy of a tourist's foreign language phrasebook. The phrasebook can contain any information that a child might wish to look up – meanings, synonyms, definitions, etc. Moreover, the phrasebook can be extended easily by the child, by using three simple commands – TEACH, FIND and FORGET. 'Teach' adds an entry to the phrasebook. Thus, TEACH 'CAT' CHAT adds the entry 'chat' to the phrasebook. FIND [CAT] would return 'chat' and FORGET [CAT] would remove the entries 'cat' and 'chat'.

The second program offered by Sharples is called 'Boxes', and is best conceptualized by imagining a series of labelled cardboard boxes into which pieces of paper bearing words or strings of words can be placed. Thus, the boxes might be called 'nouns', 'verbs', 'adjectives', 'articles', 'adverbs' with appropriate words placed in each box. The boxes might contain the following:

nouns – cat, rat, dogs, elephant, crow, whale
verbs – swims, glides, flies, waddles
adjectives – blue, speckled, pink, brown
adverbs – quickly, gracefully, happily
articles – the, a

We could then give an instruction to remove words from the boxes, following a particular order. So, for example, the order might be 'article, adjective, noun, verb, adverb', producing

'the speckled whale waddles happily'

(Recall that the words are selected at random, but the order is specified.)

This is the essence of Sharples' 'Boxes' program. Computer 'boxes' can be established, and words entered into and removed from the boxes. The boxes can have any label and any pattern selected to produce a string of words (sentence). The commands used to create boxes, to place words into boxes, to set a pattern and to generate sentences are easy to understand, as is the physical analogy.

Sharples reports successful use of the Boxes program with children aged above 10. He points out that although the sentences produced may not be grammatically or semantically correct, they focus the children's attention on the fact that words do not fall at random into sentences; that there are some patterns which are more acceptable than others, and that many levels of 'correctness' exist – syntax, semantics, tense and number agreement, appropriate use of articles. Thus, a program like 'Boxes' can be used to direct the children's attention to the significance of language as a means of expression. Although Sharples' work was carried out with children older than 10, younger children also respond well to the 'Boxes' program.

They readily conceptualize the analogy with physical boxes, and the concepts of naming boxes, adding words and establishing a pattern. They are also well able to judge the level of correctness of the program's productions. Indeed, the analogy with physical boxes is one which can be understood by children as young as 5 and 6, who are able to play a game in which they name boxes, write words, place them in the appropriate boxes and decide the order in which the words should be taken from the boxes. Further, even such young children are able to form a judgement as to the general level of 'correctness', i.e., does the sentence sound strange? If so, why does it sound strange?

Both 'Phrasebook' and 'Boxes' have many of the features of turtle geometry. They are accessed by the use of simple commands (PUT, MAKE, FORGET, FIND) which make sense to the child. Users are placed in a position of control in which they teach the computer something (new words, new meanings, etc.). Perhaps most significantly, these programs direct children's attention to ways in which language can be used to create different effects, and how language can have differing levels of 'correctness', i.e., they focus the attention on how language is structured. In this process, children have to reflect on their own understanding of language, a process further fostered by productions which are 'incorrect' at some level, for example, 'the speckled whale waddles happily' is syntactically sound, but is less acceptable semantically. The production of such a sentence can however act not just as a source of amusement, but also as a stimulation to reflect on the meanings and significance of the words, and, in so doing to reflect on the power of language to create images. Other productions could contain other types of error, for example, 'a brown dogs swims quickly' thereby encouraging consideration of the relationships between noun and verb and between article and noun. Thus, Sharples' approach also shares another important component with turtle graphics, which is that errors are expected, and act as a source of further learning.

The importance of bugs

A central component in Papert's vision of the use of Logo is that errors or 'bugs' will be made. Indeed, it can be argued that not only are errors expected but that they should be encouraged, in the sense that children should be placed in situations which challenge their existing mental structures. It is only by challenging existing mental structures that inadequacies can be revealed and development occur. The influence of Piaget predominates here. Like Piaget, Papert sees learning as a constructive process. People develop and possess different theories or models about the world as a result of their varied experiences. The greater the quality and quantity of those experiences, the richer the models will be. However, these experiences have to be active. Children are perceived as builders of their own intellectual structures, and society and culture are the sources of the raw materials. It is within such a framework that the role of errors (bugs) and error correction (debugging) need to be placed. Errors are not failings to be regarded as major inconveniences. They are an integral component of the constructive process of personal and active theory building.

The nature of the feedback provided by Logo is such that it is said to encourage the process of debugging and hence of theory construction. Thus, when the turtle does not act in a manner that the child expected or planned, this can be used as a rich source for encouraging reflection on the reasons why a different result ensued. Such a process is intensified when children have particular goals in mind. In such situations, they have a mental image of what they want the turtle to do. If the turtle does not perform in the envisaged manner there is then a mismatch between the cognitive image and the physical event. It is this discrepancy which leads to a search for an explanation. In Piagetian terms, the fact that the turtle does not behave in the anticipated manner causes a loss of equilibrium which can only be resolved by the process of accommodation in which a more sophisticated model is developed.

This can be illustrated by the process of decentring, which is the ability to perceive a situation from another's perspective. The use of the turtle requires the exercise of such a skill. Thus, when the floor turtle is facing the user or when the screen turtle

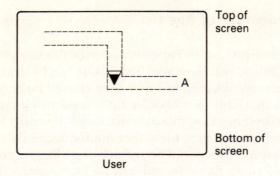

Figure 6.4

is pointing towards the bottom of the screen, the turtle's left is the user's right. So, in Figure 6.4 if the child wishes to turn the turtle to face point A (e.g., in manipulating the turtle through a maze), the turtle has to be turned to its left (the child's right).

This is a difficult decentring turn, and children of 6 and 7 experience problems with such a turn. Frequently they give a turn right instruction. It is easy to see why this should be – it is to their right. However, the interesting point is the children's reaction. They give a turn right command and will say that they expect the turtle to turn to face the target. When it turns the other way, they express surprise and puzzlement. Their hypothesis has not been confirmed – a loss of equilibrium has occurred. Such an eventuality becomes the stimulus for reflection on why the turtle has not turned as anticipated. Children will often spontaneously discuss possible reasons or can be guided to discuss reasons. In this example they might be reminded that the turtle needs 'to see where it is going', to be given small model turtles or encouraged to put themselves in the turtle's position. Such aids can help bring children to a realization that in order to control the turtle accurately, they need to be aware of the turtle's perspective. (I have known of children who have attempted to stand on their heads in order to face the same way as the screen turtle! Although perhaps not an activity we would normally want to encourage in the classroom it does indicate the potential of Logo to capture and challenge children's imagination.)

Bugs as sources of cognitive growth

The process described here is one in which apparent 'errors' are used both to provide an insight into the cognitive models held and as a means of developing those models. The use of Logo as envisaged by Papert abounds with similar examples. In the process of debugging, children are said to gain greater control and understanding of their own thinking which results in cognitive growth. Further, this is seen as having benefits which go beyond the immediate confines of Logo. Debugging is seen as general-purpose cognitive skill. In part, Logo was designed as a general cognitive tool to enable people to become reflective about their own thought processes, to see the consequences of their own thinking and to think about their thinking.

Inevitably, there are problems associated with this. These lie not in the goal of developing thinking skills which can be applied across domains – this has been a goal of educators for decades – but in how this goal can be achieved within the context of Logo. Some have understood the underlying Logo philosophy to imply free, unrestricted play and interaction with the Logo environment. Certainly, exploration and enjoyment are stressed by Papert and other Logo enthusiasts, but this does not necessarily imply that the exploration be completely open-ended. Leron (1985) writes

. . . if we adhere to the ideal of totally spontaneous, non-directed, Piagetian learning, we may find children not acquiring the powerful ideas as much as we had hoped.

Leron bases such a conclusion on his observations of 11- and 12-year-old children learning to program in Logo. He notes that under 'open' conditions the children did not make use of the powerful commands available to them, and that their activities were accompanied by little planning and reflection. His proposed solution is the provision of study guides which partially direct activities and promote children to reflect on the results of their activities. He refers to this as 'quasi-Piagetian learning' and maintains that the provision of an appropriately structured environment can enhance exploration and autonomy rather than restrict it. Psychologically, the provision of a learning environment which is cognitively accessible to the learner is less likely to lead to cognitive overload and confusion. What constitutes an appropriate environment will vary according to the level of expertise of the learners. However, broadly speaking, such environments should retain a spirit of exploration and discovery but within a framework which is within the cognitive competence and grasp of the learners. Students should feel that they can achieve the goals that they set or that are set for them. The role of debugging takes on a particular significance in such a context. If learners have a cognitive expectation that success is possible, they are more likely to strive to resolve any problems than if they feel that the problems are beyond their competence. Debugging will only be constructive and productive when the errors can be related to what the learners already know (existing models) and the solutions incorporated into those models (accommodation and cognitive restructuring).

Does Logo work?

The approach advocated by Papert and his colleagues has been associated with a considerable number of claims concerning the efficacy of Logo. By the provision of a potentially interactive learning environment in which abstract concepts can be made more concrete and then manipulated, Papert claims that children will develop more sophisticated cognitive skills than by using conventional educational technologies. This is not an insignificant claim. Papert appears to be stating that Logo contains the potential to change the nature of education and to influence cognition and cognitive development. To what extent is such a claim justified?

Broadly speaking it would have to be said that there is an absence of good evidence to support such a broad claim. Several reasons can be put forward to try to account for why this is so. In the first instance, much of the evidence cited by Papert and his immediate colleagues is of an anecdotal nature. The Logo literature abounds with reports of highly motivated and enthusiastic children who 'appear' to be gaining from their Logo programming. In many instances there is an assumption that because children are motivated and involved in an activity learning gains will invariably ensue. Although this may indeed be the case, statements of belief and anecdotes rarely satisfy educational decision makers. Despite the fact that Logo has been widely available in education for several years, reports which are little more than accounts of children's reactions continue to appear in the literature. Although these can constitute a useful starting point, they do little to elucidate what, if any, benefits accrue from using Logo.

Logo and general cognitive skills

There are, however, a number of investigators who have gone beyond this and who have attempted to investigate the claim that Logo programming can result in cognitive gains in certain areas of activity. Although there is a relative scarcity of controlled studies concerning possible benefits, several preliminary hypotheses can be established. Clements and Gullo (1984) point out that in using Logo children often develop and debug their own projects. In so doing, they establish their own goals and reflect on the nature of their thinking in attempting to turn abstract ideas into concrete representations. Further, the near inevitability of errors and the necessity for debugging is said to encourage additional self-reflection as children think about the nature of their errors and how to correct them. Given that these activities are embedded possibilities within Logo, a tentative hypothesis is that changes might occur in creativity and in a number of broad cognitive skills including reflectivity and the ability to recognize when errors have been made. In addition, it might be anticipated that because Logo involves turning abstract ideas into a concrete representation changes in abstract thinking might take place. When Clements and Gullo looked at the effects of Logo programming on such abilities they did find some evidence to suggest that experience with Logo could result in gains in creativity (divergent thinking) and in reflectivity. There was also evidence to support the contention that experience with Logo could result in an enhanced ability to monitor one's own thinking and to appreciate when one does not fully understand something. There was, however, no evidence to indicate that general cognitive development was enhanced. Clements and Gullo's paper thus seems to suggest that Logo programming can affect cognitive style (ways of thinking) and some aspects of problem solving.

In a later study, Clements (1986) again found that Logo programming resulted in gains in certain metacognitive skills, including those of deciding on the nature of a problem and on appropriate solution processes. The nature of the Logo programming environment is such that having established a goal (or been set a goal) a number of problem-solving skills come into operation in order to attain the goal. The evidence from Clements' study, and from his earlier study with Gullo, suggests that Logo might be an appropriate environment for developing the broad cognitive skills associated with such problem-solving activities. It should be noted, however, that Clements did not replicate all the findings of the earlier study. In contrast to the findings of Clements and Gullo he found no differences in reflectivity, but did find some evidence to support the contention that certain cognitive skills might be enhanced via using Logo (classification and seriation). It should also be borne in mind in trying to interpret these results that, unlike many traditional classroom settings, the children worked in small groups, with good computer resources and with the support of a computer-literate teacher.

A somewhat different approach was adopted by Pea, Kurland and Hawkins (1985) in trying to evaluate the presence of any Logo-related effects. They sought to assess whether experience with Logo would transfer to a non-computer planning activity, hypothesizing that the planning behaviour involved in Logo programming engaged a number of skills relevant to non-Logo domains, for example, defining the problem, planning a solution, implementing a plan and monitoring the plan. Over a two-year period, they found improvements with age, but no evidence to indicate that Logo experiences transferred to non-Logo activities, contrary to what might have been predicted if use of Logo enhances general problem-solving skills.

These findings are illustrative of a general pattern. Although there are welcome signs that investigations are moving away from anecdotal reports, the controlled studies which have been carried out show a lack of consistency in their findings. There are signs that experience with Logo does have some positive effects on problem-solving skills, but these are by no means consistent, nor are they of the scale suggested by the initial enthusiasm for Logo. A consequence of this is that a view has developed in both the UK and USA that Logo is neither living up to its initial promise, nor succeeding (Brock, 1988).

In defence of Logo

Evaluation

Although the picture concerning the claimed benefits of using Logo is unclear, there is an impression that many of the claims are, as yet, unsubstantiated. It would, however, be premature to conclude that the claims do not possess some validity, as a problem exists in what is being evaluated. Indeed, there is some dispute about whether Logo can be evaluated by conventional methodologies. In some quarters there seems to be a view that the conventional techniques advocated in experimental educational psychology are less informative than anecdotal accounts. Cynthia Solomon (1986), who worked with Papert's group at the Massachusetts Institute of Technology, suggests that Logo does not fit standard evaluation models. The essence of her argument is that the use of Logo, as advocated by Papert, leads to questions and interpretations of such a general nature that they cannot be answered by adopting traditional experimental methodologies. She suggests that the situation is easier when the question is not about Logo in general, but about a particular use. Thus, in order to find out if teachers find Logo to be a useful teaching aid, an appropriate methodology is to ask teachers and to rely on their professional expertise. On the other hand, if the question is one which addresses the presence of differing learning styles within Logo, observational techniques and detailed transactions of Logo sessions are appropriate. For Solomon, the problem lies with the nature of the questions which have been asked to date. She maintains that these have been predominantly influenced by traditional concerns over effectiveness, which presuppose particular investigative approaches and techniques. Her argument is that the potential Logo effects are so general that they require a different form of evaluation which depends upon the nature of the questions asked.

Logo programming experience

Peter Goodyear (1987) argues that it is premature to try to evaluate many of the Logo claims until we possess a clearer picture of the task facing the novice programmer. In essence, many of the claims associated with Logo presuppose that the programming activities promoted by the use of Logo will have beneficial cognitive effects. Thus, Nickerson (1983) writes

> . . . programming is prototypical of many cognitively demanding tasks. It is a creative endeavour requiring planning, precision in the use of language, the generation and testing of hypotheses, the ability to identify action sequences that will realize specific objectives, careful attention to detail and a variety of other skills that seem to reflect what thinking is all about.

Few would argue that such skills are indeed involved in programming, and that they are relevant to a variety of non-computer tasks. However, the description proposed by Nickerson is one which is more characteristic of an expert programmer, with many hundreds of hours of programming experience. Children learning to program in Logo are not in such a situation. They are novices in many senses of the word. Their experience of programming is severely limited, and much of their cognitive endeavour is directed towards understanding the mechanics of the language. Despite its apparent simplicity, Logo does contain a number of features which cause difficulty for young children. Fay and Mayer (1987) report that young children tend to be egocentric in their use of Logo, giving commands relating to their perception of the world and not that of the turtle. Younger children also tended to assume that a 'turn' command would make the turtle turn and move. Cohen and Geva (1986) report that children also experience problems with the wrap-round feature of Logo, the 'Repeat' command and the idea of procedure writing and debugging. Such evidence suggests that although superficially simple to use, Logo does present the user with a number of difficulties which they have to overcome before they can effectively use the language. Such analyses, which address the conceptual difficulties children may experience when using Logo, are important as they point to possible language modifications or to the need to develop more explicit tutorial strategies. If children do indeed experience some difficulty in understanding Logo and given the relatively limited amount of experience children have had in programming, it is perhaps not surprising that few studies have reported major gains or transfer effects.

Transfer of skills and 'powerful' ideas

In a not dissimilar vein, Pea, Kurland and Hawkins discuss why their study failed to show transfer from Logo experiences to a classroom planning task. They argue that although there are a number of potentially 'powerful' cognitive skills associated with the use of Logo, there is nothing within Logo which will ensure that transfer will occur or that the users will appreciate the significance of the cognition involved. They point out that Logo makes possible such activities as planning, decomposition, problem solving and debugging, but that if these activities do not possess a personal significance for the user, there is little to suggest that the power of these broad cognitive skills will be utilized in other areas. Where transfer has been reported they speculate that

. . . wherever we see children using Logo in the ways its designers hoped, and learning new thinking and problem-solving skills, it is because someone has provided guidance, support and ideas for how the language could be used.

In order to utilize Logo as a vehicle for promoting thinking and problem-solving skills they suggest that there is a

. . . need to create a culture in which students, peers and teachers talk about thinking skills and display them aloud for others to share and learn from, and that builds bridges to thinking about other domains of school and life.

The question of guidance is one also addressed by Tony Simon (1987) of Sheffield University in England. He argues that the educational philosophy of free exploratory learning espoused by Papert is insufficient to ensure that cognitive gains will ensue. He points out that previous attempts to translate Piagetian theory into educational practice have not been successful and that they tend to illustrate that open-ended, unstructured self-discovery learning rarely results in advances over traditional methods of education. Like Goodyear, Simon maintains that children's use of Logo to date has been too sparse in order for any potential transfer effects to occur. Simon, however, goes beyond the criticism of lack of experience. Drawing on an argument by Alan Newell he points out that widely applicable general problem-solving skills are not, in fact, 'powerful ideas', contrary to what seems to be implied by Papert. The reason they are not 'powerful' is because they are too general. Knowledge of the potential utility of such skills as planning or checking will not, on its own, ensure a solution to a specific problem. In order for effective thinking to occur, the general-purpose executive skills need to be coupled with a knowledge base relevant to the problem area being addressed.

Overview

There thus appear to be at least three inter-related aspects relevant to the problem of why the use of Logo has not yet realized the claims made for it. In the first instance, children have had relatively little experience of programming in Logo in comparison with 'expert' programmers. This effectively means that their cognitive energies will be used in learning the language and not in reflecting on the higher-order skills embodied within the language. Secondly, although Logo does contain the potential to encourage a number of problem-solving activities, there is nothing in the unstructured use of the language to suggest that their use will be either appreciated or will transfer to other problem domains. Finally, even if users are aware of the potential utility of such activities of planning, self-monitoring, checking, etc., their successful application to other areas needs to be coupled with a knowledge base of the area in question. The 'heart' of Papert's advocacy of Logo is that its use will lead to the natural development of general problem-solving skills, without structured intervention. Simon concludes

From all that is currently known about such processes it appears very unlikely that, except in extreme cases of genius, such development is ever likely to occur on a large scale . . .. In the face of the necessity for considerable exposure to a problem space, how likely is it that young children using Logo in an unstructured way for a few hours a week even for a few years will ever attain anything close to general problem-solving skills?

In place of the unstructured approaches often associated with Logo, Simon advocates the use of approaches derived from instructional psychology which address the related issues of

understanding and then teaching thinking skills to both children and adults. Simon's 'solution' is a structured approach
which trains the development of such higher-order skills as
planning, checking and monitoring, coupled with their application to an area with which the child is already familiar (has an
established knowledge base).

Structure and guidance in a Logo classroom

Within the Logo culture, Peter Skillen of the North York Board of
Education in Toronto has gone some way towards implementing an approach which bears a number of similarities to
that advocated by Tony Simon. Skillen (1986) neatly encapsulates much of the discussion relating to the use of Logo by
quoting from Corinthians

> Everything is permissible,
> But not everything is beneficial.
>
> Everything is permissible,
> But not everything is constructive.

Skillen's concern is to identify Logo activities which are both
beneficial and constructive. In particular, he argues that Logo
was designed as a tool for thinking in which people could
become more aware and reflective about their own thought
processes. His aim is thus that of helping students discover
knowledge about knowledge as a means of enhancing the
development of domain-independent skills. This aim is not
dissimilar from those generally associated with Logo. However,
Skillen places it within a context of how it might be achieved
within the classroom environment by focusing on the potentially constructive nature of bugs. As outlined earlier, bugs are an
inherent component of Logo activities and provide an insight
into the nature of what the student knows and doesn't know.
His methodology involves encouraging students to look for
errors in their own Logo activities. He writes

Children soon got used to the idea of having bugs in their program. These were
not bad things – rather they were things to be fixed.

The search for bugs became a game; bug collections were

established, and, as difficulties (bugs) were solved, imaginary bugs were fed to a model turtle in the classroom. There is little doubt that the methodology described involves reflection on one's own thinking. However, perhaps the most significant observation reported by him is that

The children started looking for bugs elsewhere in their classroom lives . . ..
They would actively seek mistakes in their math, spelling, reading and so on.
An unusual situation for a classroom one must admit! What a refreshing change to see young excited learners revelling in learning from their mistakes – rather than being ashamed of them.

This approach thus goes some way to satisfying some of the criticisms raised earlier. There is guidance in encouraging the search for errors; this involves the exercise of the higher-order executive skills of self-reflection and monitoring, which are then applied to other areas in the curriculum. Unfortunately, to date, this work has been mainly anecdotal. However, the approach is an advance on the earlier unstructured methodologies associated with Logo. It offers a framework for the implementation and observation of Logo activities and associated cognitive skills. Further research should clarify whether the apparent gains claimed are, in fact, occurring.

Conclusion

There is little doubt that Logo is likely to remain an important component of the educational computing scene. However, Papert's vision of a transformed educational environment has been modified in the light of practical experience. Rather than attempting to evaluate such broad questions as 'Is Logo successful in teaching problem-solving skills to children?' researchers are increasingly directing their attention to specific and well-defined questions about the use of Logo. Issues raised concern the difficulties children experience in using Logo; the amount of experience required to go beyond the level of 'novice' programmer; what skills are used; how best to facilitate transfer, and the extent to which guidance and supporting materials are necessary for the effective use of Logo. The success or otherwise of Logo will ultimately depend on the extent to which research can provide answers to the problems and questions which have been raised. Like other educational resources, Logo is a tool, and like all tools its optimum use depends on knowing how and when to use it, and for which tasks it is most suitable.

7   *The Release of Trapped Intelligence*

Use of Technology with Communication-impaired Children

A major theme throughout this book is that technology can be utilized to aid and enhance the development and expression of underlying cognitive skills. Central to this concept is that such a fostering of cognition is facilitated when individuals are given the opportunity to explore their own thinking through interaction and communication with suitably designed learning environments. This, essentially, is a development of the view that humans are active, rather than passive, processors of information and that human cognition is more adequately explained by such a viewpoint.

The enabling technology

There are, however, individuals for whom active control and influence over the environment present considerable problems. Thus, a unifying feature of many handicapping conditions concerns the extent to which active control is restricted, both by the nature of the impairment and, in many cases, by the surrounding environment which may impose passivity on an individual. For such individuals, rather than being integral components of everyday life interaction and communication become sources of difficulty and anxiety – often things to avoid rather than seek out. Within this field it has become somewhat of a convention to regard modern technology, and particularly the microcomputer, as an 'enabling technology' in that it can

144

reduce many of the demands and restrictions placed upon handicapped individuals, freeing them for other activities. Frequently, this 'enablement' is perceived in the context of the provision of improved prostheses, for example, scanning devices, mobility aids, input devices, control switches, which make it possible for a disabled individual to interact more fully with the environment. Hawkridge, Vincent and Hales (1985) document many examples of technology being utilized in such a manner. The application of technology to act as an interface between the individual and the world has resulted in many dramatic examples which illustrate the potential of the technology to act in a liberating manner. In one of the most celebrated examples, Weir (1981) describes the case of an adolescent suffering from cerebral palsy involving all four limbs with an associated speech defect. The fact that cerebral palsy affects the output side of human performance means that conventional testing and assessment procedures are difficult to administer resulting in problems in the accurate evaluation of an individual's potential. In the case described by Weir, the provision of an appropriate performance environment (Logo with a simplified control system for use by the physically handicapped) resulted in the release of what Weir termed 'trapped intelligence'. In this case, a student who had presented major classroom management problems was able to demonstrate considerable academic potential as a result of technological intervention. Such was this student's potential that he eventually went on to be a successful university student. More recently, Weir (1987) has described in detail some of her work using Logo with children experiencing a range of disabling conditions. In a similar vein, Paul Goldenberg (1979, 1984) has provided convincing evidence of the potential power of computer applications to enable children with special educational needs (autism, physical handicap, auditory impairments) to exhibit skills and abilities which had not been demonstrated under conventional classroom conditions. The success of such work illustrates the important distinction between performance and cognitive capacity, and that the former may be a poor guide to the latter. Although this has been raised in the context of the application of technology to special-needs groups, it should be pointed out that the distinction was implied by researchers in the field of special education for many years (see Clarke and Hermelin, 1955, and Bortner and Birch, 1970), where the restructuring of tasks enabled mentally handicapped adults to display new skills revealing unsuspected abilities.

In such examples, the expression of hidden abilities was not consequent upon any change in the individual, but followed changes which made the environment more accessible to the individual. There are strong reasons to argue that an appropriate role for modern educational technology is to provide an extension of the learning environments available and accessible to the learner. This may be accomplished by improvements in technique or by the provision of suitable hardware or software – the principle is the same in each case.

The practical model of 'enabling technology' is thus one in which the environment is made more accessible to the learner, either by a restructuring of that environment, or by providing a means to allow the learner to interact more fully with the environment, or most effectively, by a combination of these two aspects. Technology, in many of its guises, is therefore placed in the role of being the interface between the user and the environment. In other words, technology is a means, and not an end in itself. It possesses the potential to act as a releaser for a range of cognitive skills as well as assisting in the development of new skills.

We should not, however, assume that simply providing access to technology via a suitable interface will invariably result in the development of enhanced skills. The application of technology should be guided by an educational philosophy which recognizes the importance of communication and the role of computers as communication devices.

Significance of communication

Learning of any kind involves communication between the learner and the surrounding environment. Within the cognitive approach, information is taken in via the sensory receptors (sight, sound, touch, smell), is transformed, given meaning and reacted to. Communication thus involves receiving, transforming and sending information in a process of interaction with the world. Thus,

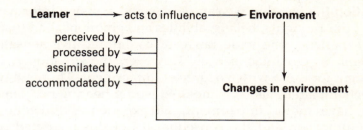

Via this process the learner establishes mental models as a result of interactions involving both initiated actions and perceived, meaningful feedback. The schemata developed serve to direct future actions and to act as guidelines for behaviour.

Within this framework, communication plays a central role as it is via communication that learners influence the environment and also indicate the nature of their underlying mental models. Note that here, communication does not imply just speech – it implies all the means by which we interact with the world – facial expression, gesture, as well as vocal utterances, together with all our means of receiving information.

Effective communication thus requires reliable means of receiving input and making output. Clearly, children who experience difficulty in either reception or expression will also experience difficulty in communication. There is a unifying theme which links most areas of disability, which is that one consequence of disability is a reduction in both the quality and quantity of interaction available to the individual. Hawkridge *et al.* (1985) express it thus

For many disabled people, communication problems are at the heart of their disablement and central to their personal struggle to learn to overcome their disabilities . . .. They are often left isolated, powerless and dependent. They are deprived of important ways of expressing their individuality.

Consequences of restricted communication

Although the differing categories of handicap (motor, visual, auditory, speech, cognitive) show unique patterns of disability, often requiring specific forms of remedial treatment, underlying all categories is a restriction in the nature of interaction between the individual and the world. Most of us accept without question the fact that we can receive and transmit information about our thoughts, beliefs, abilities and emotions, and that we can experience the wide range of communicative sensations available to our intact senses. However, the situation is very different for those with a degree of impairment. Those who are speech impaired, visually impaired, suffer hearing problems or who have motor impairment, all experience difficulties in communication and the consequences of this restricted communication can be profound. Motor-impaired children cannot explore their world and manipulate everyday objects with the same ease as can non-impaired children. They may be unable to reach and grasp objects, therefore finding it impossible to play with building bricks, jigsaws and construction sets. This lack of motor experience not only affects the quality of life experienced by such children, but also may adversely affect the development of certain cognitive skills involving spatial understanding.

Children who suffer early hearing impairment suffer from considerably more than difficulties in enunciating words. Their whole auditory world is restricted and the consequences affect the entire structure of language perception and comprehension. Evidence from around the world on the linguistic development of hearing impaired children indicates that on average they lag several years behind their hearing counterparts in terms of linguistic skills.

A lack of interaction and communication with the environment means that a handicapped child is essentially deprived of environmental range and variation. The difficulties experienced in this respect by the sensory and motor handicapped are apparent. Less obviously, those with learning disabilities face similar problems in that they experience difficulties in processing and making sense of the range of information experienced.

Theoretical considerations

Ulrich Neisser (1967) has argued that in a normal environment, objects and events possess implications for those in that environment. Neisser argues that individuals acquire know-ledge and understanding from their interactions with their environments and that ultimately, experience and interaction are at the basis of the development of knowledge and under-standing. Clearly, if one's degree of interaction with the environment is restricted then the acquisition of knowledge and understanding will be retarded.

Although Neisser's is a general statement, common to most models of cognitive development, it can be made more specific. Central to many theories of cognitive growth is the hypothesis that early motor experience is the foundation-stone upon which intellectual development is built. Where motor problems exists, such theories predict that cognitive growth will be affected. A major influence in the development of such theories is Piaget (see Chapter 4). As described earlier, Piaget's theory suggests that a child's development of cognitive skills passes through a well-defined sequence of stages, with each stage indicating what the child can or cannot do. A corner-stone of the theory would appear to be that self-initiated actions and experiences form the basis of mental growth. As the child moves away from the dictates of immediate experience so progression to mental maturity occurs. Where self-initiated actions and experiences are lacking or limited, then that progression will be adversely affected. So, for example, the child is seen as first co-ordinating motor actions, then mental representations of these actions, and then sequences of mental operations. Thus, abstract knowledge appears to be traced directly back to physical action. Kephart (1971) writes

Through these first motor explorations the child begins first to find out about himself, then the world around him, and his motor experimentation and his motor learning become the foundation-stone upon which such knowledge is built.

A similar view is encompassed by Piaget's (1971) statement that 'knowledge is derived from action'. Within education, such statements as 'Children do not learn by sitting passively in their seats . . .' (Pulaski, 1971) and 'the pre-school child . . . should be given tasks that allow him to act on objects' (Ault, 1977) can be seen as being in accordance with such a viewpoint. Clearly, within such a framework, children who experience a restricted degree of control over the environment seem destined to experience cognitive difficulties. Despite this apparently gloomy prognosis, there are well-documented instances of severely motor impaired individuals who are cognitively very able. The presence of such individuals must raise questions about the precise relationship of motor activity to cognitive growth.

In general, there is little direct evidence concerning the interaction of severity of motor impairment with cognitive expression. If the IQs of cerebral-palsied individuals are taken as a guide, it is clear that, overall, this group scores lower than non-impaired individuals. Such evidence, however, does not necessarily support the view that motor impairment will invariably lead to cognitive impairment, since low IQs in cerebral-palsied children may relate to the brain damage underlying the motor problem rather than to the motor problem itself. More significantly, Zeitschel *et al.* (1979) have demonstrated that cerebral-palsied individuals score lower on tests of visual perception when the test has a high motor component than when there is no motor component. Similar improvements in performance when the motor element is removed have been reported by Bortner and Birch (1962), suggesting that the problem lies in the motor act itself and not in the underlying cognition.

Meaning of 'action'

Such examples lead one to conclude that the hypothesis that motor action is the foundation stone on which cognition is based is an over-simplification. Neisser's view is that our extraction of information from a situation depends on '. . . the individual's control of information pick-up'. In Neisser's terms, interpretation of meaning (central to understanding) depends upon the activated schemata. For example, whether I process an individual's arm movement as simply 'someone moving an arm', 'someone greeting me' or 'someone waving a fist at me' depends upon whether I expect to meet someone, whether I may have caused annoyance, etc. In other words, my interpretation depends on being able to extract meaning from a situation.

This, in turn, depends on previously acquired and processed information.

Experience and interaction with the environment thus affect the development of schemata. Neisser refers to the development of schemata through 'information pick up'. Thus, individuals extract knowledge through acquiring information about situations. If the means by which information is acquired are disrupted, then, inevitably, the acquisition of knowledge will also be disrupted. One source of disruption is, as indicated, motor disruption. However, other disabling conditions also involve a disruption of the normal process of interaction. It can be argued that it is not motor movement *per se* that contributes to cognitive development, but the opportunity motor movement normally provides to link actions with consequences, to connect cause and effect, to develop schemata. Lack of interaction, not lack of movement, may more severely restrict cognitive growth. It may be that those severely motor-impaired individuals who have developed good cognitive skills have achieved, in some way, a degree of consistent control over their environments via a modality other than motor movement.

Importance of feedback

The basis of such control is the feedback the individual receives from the world concerning the consequences of 'actions', and future performances are modified on the basis of this feedback. If action/control is lacking, or if feedback is absent, restricted or distorted, then learning will be impaired. The interpretation of action is that it incorporates the notion of active involvement with the environment, i.e., if an individual is able to exercise some form of self-initiated control over the environment then cognitive potential may be optimized. A major problem experienced by the disabled is that such control and feedback are frequently distorted or absent. Thus, the motor handicapped lack motor control and motor feedback; the hearing-impaired are restricted in their linguistic control, and the learning-impaired are limited in their ability to extract and process meanings and implications from the environment.

The significance of such control is emphasized by the psychological approaches of Bower (1979), Vygotsky (1978) and Bruner (1966). In the present context, the principal aim is to enable a disabled child to exercise control and to perceive the consequences of that control.

Effect of restricted communication on personal development

In addition to the more apparent adverse consequences of restricted communication upon a range of cognitive skills, limited communication also implies a restriction in social development. In many senses, human beings are social organisms. We rely on our families, friends and colleagues for a wide range of our everyday activities – simple conversations, jokes, shared interests, leisure pursuits. Most of these activities involve our ability to communicate. Restrictions in this ability will inevitably limit the range of social activities made possible.

The problem, however, extends beyond cognitive and social consequences. I recall being present in a classroom of hearing-impaired children when they were required to carry out some work in written English. Their reaction was one of distress and lack of motivation and interest. They did not wish to read, nor did they wish to write. Contrast this with the same group of children several minutes later when asked to demonstrate on the blackboard how to work out some quite complex arithmetic tasks. A forest of hands shot into the air. There was enthusiasm and commitment, and a considerable degree of ability. Two commonplace classroom activities, presented to the same children within the space of 30 minutes, both requiring the exercise of cognitive skills, both apparently equally difficult, yet drawing forth reactions of extreme contrast. Anxiety and avoidance for one task, enthusiasm and motivation for the other. Obviously, the English-language task required the use of skills at which hearing-impaired children are generally rather poor and *the children were aware of their problems with such tasks*. The arithmetic task does not involve linguistic skills, and so hearing-impaired children have an opportunity to demonstrate what they can do, rather than what they cannot do. When I spoke to the teacher,

her comment was 'At English, they have a history of difficulty and of losing. At arithmetic they can be winners.'

This statement contains very significant implications, as it relates to the way in which individuals evaluate their performance and their expectancies of future performance. A central aspect is that individuals possess, amongst other things, a set of cognitions about themselves, their abilities, their relationships and their interactions with the environment, and that these perceptions influence behaviour. Negative experiences and evaluations on a task can have deleterious effects on future motivation for carrying out that task. In essence, the argument is that a history of failure will adversely influence the perception of one's own abilities when faced with future challenges. Bandura (1977) has emphasized the importance of self-efficacy – the belief that one is able to control one's own life and deal with challenges. Within this is the idea that individuals with positive self-efficacy possess self-confidence that they can deal with life's challenges. The other side of the coin is the notion of learned helplessness, in which there is an assumption within the individual that success is not possible. For such individuals, avoidance of challenge can become a way of life, with predictable consequences on cognition and emotional development.

Implications

These concepts have significant implications when placed within the context of handicap. As indicated above, a common theme in disability is that of restricted interactivity. This restricted interactivity also frequently involves a passive mode of existence rather than an active one. The nature of the disability may be such that passivity and dependence on others becomes incorporated into everyday life, and the child is able to exercise little direct control over the surrounding world. Within the cognitive model espoused here, this lack of self-initiated control has implications for cognitive growth. Moreover, within the framework of cognitive evaluation and expectancy, extreme passivity may result in a form of learned helplessness together with a pattern of low expectations. The low expectations may exist both within the individual and within those surrounding that person, with the inevitable result that he or she is rarely placed in a situation where personal control can be exercised in a manner that can lead to success and to positive self-image.

In discussing the use of computers with children, Papert draws a distinction between the computer programming the child, and the child programming the computer – between passive and active modes of control. In many senses, the situation is exaggerated for many disabled individuals. The nature of their disability is such that the environment controls them; this can become more pronounced when individuals are institutionalized. A common observation relates to the passivity experienced by many disabled children. An equally common comment is that we need to provide opportunities to break out of such passivity; that we need to shift the locus of control away from the environment and towards the individual. The advent of computer technology provides a means to achieve this goal. By the use of suitable interfaces, many disabled individuals can now exercise a degree of control which would otherwise have been impossible. The locus of control can be shifted, and the consequences for our understanding of underlying capabilities may be profound. We thus have a situation in which restrictions in communication have profound consequences upon an individual's ability to interact with the world, with consequences on cognitive, social and self development. This can be represented in the following way:

Disability and communication problems

leading to

Limited interaction in general

leading to

**Limited educational
opportunities**   **Limited social
interactions**

leading to

**Inadequate internal models and low
expectancies both of self and from others**

The history of our attitudes towards disability has included a concentration upon the nature of the difficulties experienced, i.e., upon what cannot be done. Although technology is not yet at a point where the disability itself can be treated, we can utilize the technology to offset some of the consequences. One major consequence has been a lack of interaction and communication – a restriction in the range of experiences that most people take for granted. We tend to overlook the significance of the everyday experiences of play and social communication, and in so doing we ignore their importance. To quote Goldenberg (1979)

It is so difficult to imagine not having had all the normal experiences – in fact, we are so totally unaware of them that it is difficult even to list them – that we may frequently interpret a handicapped child's failure to comprehend as a lack of intellectual capacity rather than a lack of information.

A major role for technology can be to act as a means to enable communicatively impaired children (and adults) to interact with the world in such a way so as to experience as wide a range of 'normal' experiences as possible. This is not an instance of seeking to 'normalize' the child but of trying to normalize the experiences. Central to cognitive and social growth are play, communication and challenge. For many handicapped children, such apparently 'normal' experiences have not been part of their life. We need to utilize the power and flexibility of the technology to make those things possible, and to provide environments in which cognitive and personal growth can take place, and in which autonomy can be developed. Simply providing suitable interfaces to enable communication to take place is a start, but, on its own, is not sufficient. It is also important to consider the nature of the environments and that of the interactions made possible.

The nature of computer-based environments for the communicatively impaired

The arguments presented above can be summarized by stating that restricted communication is seen as being at the heart of many disabilities. This restriction, involving limited interactions with the surrounding environment, has an impact on the development of an individual's internal models (schemata) which further reduces the interactions. This has consequences for the development of cognitive, social and personal skills. The implications of such an analysis for the design of computer-based intervention are clear. It is important to provide environments which enable an individual to break out of the cycle of restricted communication, which promote interactivity and which enable an active and positive role to be adopted by the individual.

Although modern technology can act as an enabling technology in the context of extending the range of experiences and interactions available to the disabled, this, in itself, is insufficient. If we consider how a non-impaired child comes to learn, it is apparent that much learning occurs in informal settings outside the confines of the classroom. An obvious example of this is the hearing child's acquisition of language. A child's early years are filled with sound – from parents, siblings, radio, TV, etc. Surrounded by language, most hearing children rapidly gain knowledge and mastery of conventional language. This enables them to ask questions, express opinions and wishes, and to discover more about their surroundings. In a sense, language is a biological enabling technology in that it makes possible many things which would otherwise be impossible. Perhaps less obviously, the everyday manipulation of objects gives a non-impaired child control over the immediate environment. From simple play activities come informal knowledge of spatial relationships and positional and relational concepts. In a more formal sense, what is argued here is that children build models of the world as a result of their experiences with the world. Piaget has expressed this by viewing children as builders of their own intellectual structures. Children seem to be gifted learners, acquiring a vast quantity of knowledge before they go to school. As already indicated, if children are unable to experience the world, their intellectual development is likely to be restricted. To use the building analogy implied above, the environment, in all its aspects, provides the materials for building cognitive structures. If one is unable to access that environment, then the raw materials for growth will not be used. What is required in the context of communication impairment is not only a means to access these materials, but also to ensure that the appropriate materials are provided to enable intellectual development to occur. The pre-school non-handicapped child has easy access to such materials without our having consciously to structure the experiences, although we may seek to assist by providing educational toys, games and exercises. The handicapped, however, are not in such a privileged position. They are often deprived of both access to the environment and access to the materials which would assist their cognitive growth. Goldenberg argues that an appropriate role for modern technology is to help normalize the range of experiences available to handicapped children, not to normalize the child. The nature of handicap is such that even the most sophisticated technological intervention cannot fully equate the range of experiences available to a handicapped child with those experienced by the non-impaired. What is possible, however, is to provide the disabled child with environments which are analogies or 'models' of normal environments. Such environments can provide the disabled with access to important ideas more readily than a real-world equivalent. In other words we should seek to provide a range of experiences and opportunities from which knowledge and understanding can be extracted. Within this framework a child can operate on the environment and can perceive the consequences of those operations. This is what is meant by environmental interaction.

Sloman's (1978) view of the computer as a powerful toy is again pertinent. Within the cognitive model of learning advocated here, we can see the significance of the word 'toy'. In a sense toys are needed: objects of learning which are motivating, which allow the user a degree of autonomy, which are personal and informal. The more that educationally significant concepts can be conveyed by such toys, the less restricted the environment will be. The notion of 'restricted world' has obvious relevance within special education because of the restrictions in communication. Technology can provide an otherwise perhaps unavailable opportunity for communication with a meaningful environment.

The importance of accessibility

The notion of interaction and schematic development implies that the nature of learning depends on both the learning environment and upon the present cognitive state of the learner, which defines the operations which can be carried out on the environment. More specifically, it depends upon the matching of the two. Designing learning materials implies not just a careful analysis of task structures but also a close attention to individual differences. What a learner gains from a situation depends on making a task appropriate to current schemata: information must be within reach (accessible) of current mental models in order for that information to be processed efficiently. The learner must be able to carry out operations on the learning material, but at the same time the task should serve to display some of the weaknesses or limitations of the strategies the learner uses. All too frequently we underestimate what impaired individuals can do. In so doing, we do a disservice both to their self-esteem and to their potential cognitive growth. If we underestimate potential, we can be tempted to provide learning experiences which are too simple, which do not offer a cognitive challenge, which do not require the learner to 'struggle' to gain a deeper level of understanding, and which thereby fail to stimulate cognitive growth. This concept of 'cognitive struggle' is central to theories of cognitive development. Without it we fail to master our environments and develop our understanding. It is part of the model used here that struggle – not in the sense of encountering insurmountable difficulties, but in the sense of applying effort to understand a potentially significant environment – is essential for learning. As one parent of a learning-impaired adolescent said to me: 'I know he's not an intellectual giant, but he has the *right* to find things difficult so that he can find things out.'

Accessibility thus implies more than simply providing direct physical access to, or control over, the immediate environment. As used here, it refers to cognitive accessibility, which implies providing environments which 'make sense'. Failure to make learning situations thus 'accessible' to the present cognitive state of learners has resulted in serious misconceptions about the potential abilities of individuals. Margaret Donaldson (1978) refers to a number of studies, dealing with Piagetian tasks, which suggest similar conclusions. The common theme of these studies is the need to construct activities which make sense to children, i.e., which are not alien to their experiences, are related to knowledge of the world, and are in tune with their expectations and motivations.

Examples of accessibility

Two related examples will illustrate the importance of providing activities which make 'human sense' to a child if we are to gain an insight into cognitive functioning and potential.

One of the dominant themes of modern developmental psychology has been that despite Piaget's major influence, his emphasis on what children could *not* do at certain stages of development resulted in an under-estimation of potential. A classic illustration of this is the 'three mountains' task. In this activity, the child sits at a table on which is placed a model of three mountains. The experimenter places a doll at various positions around the table, and the task for the child is: 'What can the doll see?' The child may select one from a number of alternative pictures of the scene or may rearrange the model to represent the child's view. Piaget reported that there is a reliable tendency for children under 6 to choose a picture or model which represents what they can see and not what the doll can see, and this was taken as evidence for the children's inability to form a mental image of a view they could not actually see. However, there is good reason to believe that such a conclusion is premature. Martin Hughes (1975) carried out a similar task of 'egocentricity', but using a rather different task. The task was one which involved a social situation with everyday characters, but was one which could only be solved by perceiving a situation from another perspective. The cognitive requirements of the task were similar, yet Hughes obtained 90 per cent correct responses in a group of children aged between 3½ and 5 years. In a further study, Hughes utilized a simplified version of Piaget's 'mountains' task, and by carefully structuring the presentation of the task was able to secure a high percentage of correct responses from pre-school children. It seems that the children in Piaget's experiments did not fail to reason; rather they failed to understand.

An example from Sylvia Weir's work (1987) also illustrates the point. She reports the case of a 13-year-old quadraplegic who was presented with a version of Piaget's topographical task, conceptually similar to the 'three mountains' task. In this task, the child and experimenter had identical models of the same scene. The task for the child was to place a doll in the same position as another doll on the experimenter's model. Weir reports that when both models were the same way round, the child experienced little difficulty. However, when the experimenter turned his model round, and then asked the child to place the doll in the same position, performance was poor. Superficially, this appears to illustrate the existence of an inability to handle spatial concepts. However, when the student worked on a screen representation of the experimenter's model, performance improved dramatically. In this version, the student no longer had to place the doll physically. A screen representation could be moved by simple cursor control. When the task was carried out on the computer, the motor aspect of the activity was removed, and the student could concentrate on the essential cognitive requirements of the task and not on the problems of physically moving the doll.

Our understanding of the development of children's minds emphasizes the importance of active interaction with the environment. This is something which many disabled children find difficult, but is also an aspect which technology has the potential to circumvent. The flexibility offered by modern technology makes it a perfect extension for a child who is not flexible. Through the appropriate application of technology we can provide the child with new opportunities for stimulation building on behaviours the child normally exhibits.

Goldenberg (1979) proposes that

. . . we can best serve the human being who comes to us for help by trying to remove barriers to his experiences, thus making room for him to develop his own adaptive and integrative abilities – room for him to develop autonomy.

Autonomy is often reduced for the disabled. Technology can act to serve as a means to provide opportunities to develop such autonomy.

Theory and practice

Although such implications appear to be clear, transferring them into practice is less straightforward. The history of the relationship between theory and practice in education is one in which dogmatic assertions from the theoretician are greeted with understandable scepticism from the practitioner, who may have witnessed the rise and fall of several much-heralded educational innovations. Such a problem becomes particularly acute in situations where learners have a condition which impairs learning and where opportunity exists to structure learning by the use of powerful educational technologies. When considering the use of computer technology with the disabled both these conditions apply. The danger is one in which the application of the technology may result in a perpetuation of the passive mode of learning which may be present amongst many disabled children but which is at odds with our understanding of social, emotional and cognitive growth. Although a considerable amount of software has been produced for learning-impaired children, inspection of much of this material reveals that it is dominated by drill and practice and rote learning, with the inevitable consequence that children are again placed in a passive role. Although drill approaches can play an important part in the development of automaticity, assisting in the rehearsal of lower-level skills which will form the basis of higher-order activities, it is a severely limited approach to adopt in the context of such a powerful and flexible educational tool as the computer. Programs written in what can be termed a drill vein tend to have three major flaws. First, they lack important interactive qualities and give little informative feedback, with the learner remaining quite passive. Second, they present a limited environment which allows few opportunities for the user to take the initiative and to take part in exploratory activities. Finally, and perhaps most significantly, since it encompasses both previous points, such materials are rarely designed according to the actual needs and abilities of users who, as people with communication disabilities, require structured situations where they can engage in meaningful interactions.

Such considerations have particular significance when placed in the context of special needs education. For example, children with learning difficulties commonly demonstrate low motivation and lack of attention on conventional classroom activities, especially when these are placed in an artificial or unfamiliar context which has no relevance to the child. This can be illustrated by a report of learning-disabled children who could not carry out simple standard sequencing tasks, but who could recall, after several weeks, the sequence of operations necessary to switch on a computer, load the disc into the disc drive, load the program from disc and then carry out, from memory, the tasks required to play a computer game. (Personal communication from a Canadian teacher of the trainable mentally retarded.) This latter 'task' contains the essential operations of a sequencing activity, but differs from traditional 'tests' in that the child carries out the operations in order to achieve a self-imposed, self-motivated goal and not one which is externally imposed.

In a similar vein, Weir reports the example of a 13-year-old cerebral-palsied girl who was apparently unable to use simple 'forward', 'right', 'left' controls to manipulate the screen turtle to a target destination. However, when the task was embedded within another context, performance improved dramatically. In this case, the child selected cartoon characters from her favourite TV shows, and personalized the task by having the turtle visit the characters within her own story scenario. Several aspects are worthy of comment here. Again, we have an instance of performance being a poor guide to capacity. However, in this example, the provision of the initial computer-based activity does not result in the demonstration of 'trapped intelligence'. It is the modification of the task to make it fit in with the child's interests and motivations which results in the demonstration of improved performance. The task attained a personal salience in which she was able to draw on personal knowledge and abilities in order to succeed at an activity which had previously caused considerable difficulty.

Such examples confirm the double-edged nature of accessibility. The 'enabling technology' can provide direct physical access to otherwise inaccessible situations. However, equally significantly, it can help establish cognitive accessibility, via the application of appropriate educational techniques implemented using the technology. An appropriate role for modern technology is an extension of the learning environments available to the learner. Lumsdaine (1964) sees educational technology as being both:

1. Concerned with the use of equipment (as opposed to humans) in the teaching process (the hardware or product aspect of technology).
2. Concerned with the development of learning experiences, through the application of the sciences of learning (the software or 'process' aspect of technology).

Application of educational technology

Educational technology thus consists of the appliance of scientific results and theories in the service of education. In special education, the use of structured training programmes, derived from psychological models, resulted in dramatic revisions in our estimates of the capabilities of severely learning impaired individuals (Clarke and Hermelin, 1955). In terms of the present schematic model of learning, a learning environment needs to be brought within range of an individual's schemata. Problems of motor, sensory or cognitive functioning possess a unity in that they imply a degraded quality of interaction with the environment. Changing the environment in order to make it more accessible to the learner will enable that learner to interact more fully.

Technology can act in a particularly powerful manner to become an 'enabling' device in this context. The work already referred to illustrates this process of enablement via technological intervention in action. What is involved here is the application of theories derived from mainstream psychology to the problems of communication impairment. The application of these models can have significant consequences across a wide range of disabling conditions. The work of Weir and Goldenberg illustrates how the appropriate use of technology to enhance communication and interaction resulted in reassessment of the capabilities of physically impaired children. The power of the approach is, however, not restricted to situations where there is a belief that intelligence is 'trapped', waiting to be released.

Our children can't do that!

Rostron and Lovett (1981) report on the use of the interactive model with some of the most severely affected children. These children have been variously described in the literature as 'crucial crib cases' (Killian, 1967) and 'nonambulatory, profoundly mentally retarded, multiply handicapped' (Murphy and Doughty, 1977). Landesman-Dwyer (1974) lists seven defining characteristics of the group – extreme limited responsiveness to external stimulation; obvious severe muscular dysfunction; inability to move other than by simple turning; inability to attain or maintain a seated position; poor head control; abnormally small body size, and records indicating a 'hopeless' prognosis for behavioural and physiological development, even with treatment. It is appropriate to consider the nature of Rostron and Lovett's work as it highlights how the model discussed in this chapter can be applied successfully to even the most severely impaired children.

Observations of children in the group leave a lasting impression. The nature of their disabilities is such that interaction with the environment becomes virtually impossible. There is an absence of motor control and movement, a lack of manipulation skills, lack of verbalization and an extreme passivity. As Rostron and Lovett express it

. . . as the children spend longer and longer in this state, the lack of responsiveness becomes self-perpetuating, preventing further development and learning.

The approach they adopted to offset this passivity was to develop very simple control devices which enabled the children to exercise some degree of control over the environment. Target behaviours (e.g., simple limb or head movement, pressure on a grip-switch, blow-suck control) were reinforced using standard operant techniques with environmental responses including auditory, visual and movement rewards. The basic philosophy behind the approach adopted has been to provide aids which gave the children the potential actively to control and to interact with their surroundings and to extend the range of experiences available to them. The work carried out indicated that simple learning did take place in a group of children previously believed to be incapable of learning and of establishing cause–effect relationships. This work has been further developed by Andrew Rostron in the development of a computer-controlled 'buggy' for use with very severely motor and cognitively impaired children. This contains a variety of control options (simple switches, ultra-sonic beam, blow-suck control, pressure switches) which enable the individual to control the movement of the buggy, for example, breaking an ultra-sonic beam with a simple motor movement results in the buggy moving forward for a pre-determined time. In this situation, the individual is in a position of active control – not the passive recipient of stimuli. By the judicious use of different controls, it is possible to build up a sequence of motor movements which can be used in other situations. Thus, for example, one child who used first the beam breaking option and then grip-switch to control the buggy was subsequently observed to reach out for and grasp an object in front of her on a table. This was the first occasion on which such a behaviour had been seen. The degree of impairment experienced by these children is so extensive that such apparently simple actions have often been considered to be beyond them.

Phil Odor (1988) at the Communication Aids for Language and Learning Centre in Edinburgh has adapted and modified the approach used by Rostron in the development of a 'smart' wheelchair. Working mainly with cerebral-palsied children – cognitively considerably more able than Rostron's group – the chair is designed to facilitate conscious choice and autonomy. The provision of simple control systems, similar to those developed by Rostron, enables the child to exercise such autonomy.

In both the above cases, technology is being used as a genuine enabling device, offering children the opportunity to carry out actions and behaviours they could otherwise not experience. Such devices are considerably more than mobility aids. They are aids to cognitive and social development, providing the users with the opportunity both to exhibit and to develop previously unexpressed skills. The approaches adopted by Rostron and by Odor share many similarities with the work of Paul Goldenberg and Sylvia Weir already referred to, with an emphasis on interactivity. Nor is this basic approach restricted to enhancing control for the physically impaired. Geoffrion and Goldenberg

(1981) provide examples of communication with disabled children using interactive communication devices and stress the significance of providing interactive environments, and Ward (1989) documents the development of interactive language software for use with language-impaired children.

The basis of Ward's work lies in the application of an interactive approach to language development influenced by the work of both Halliday (1975) and Bruner (1983). In Ward's 'natural language environments' communication-impaired pupils are able to enter a restricted, but purposeful, dialogue concerning a graphics environment presented on the screen. The language available enables them to manipulate screen objects, pose and respond to questions, provide descriptions and to give instructions. Although the language available is restricted, Ward's analyses indicate significant gains in language skills following experience on his computer-based activities. Work by other members of the Hull group (Sewell and Rotheray, 1987) has illustrated the application of this principle in developing software for severely learning-impaired children. Using speech synthesis, together with screen graphics, Rotheray and Sewell have reported the development of a suite of software which enables such children to progress from simple cause–effect relationships to the exercise of problem-solving activities requiring information-handling abilities, memory skills and logical thinking. Guiding the development of this software was an approach which combined instructional design and cognitive learning theories, in which the requirements of specific tasks depended on the exercise of skills embodied within the software. The software was designed following a hierarchical task analysis which identified the essential prerequisite cognitive skills at each level within the learning hierarchy. The 'target' end behaviour was for the learner to participate in a computer-mediated game involving multiple concepts, the use of question-and-answer skills and the application of simple memory and search activities. Children who initially experienced difficulty on single-concept matching tasks (e.g., shape) were able to progress through the hierarchy to participate successfully in an activity which many of their teachers had judged to be beyond their capabilities. A distinguishing feature of this material, as with the software developed by Ward, is that its design principles derive directly from the application of cognitive and instructional theories to the cognitive and communication problems experienced by the intended users.

Conclusion

The purpose of this discussion is not to debate in detail the nature of the work referred to in the previous paragraphs. What characterizes it is that it embodies an approach in which the implications of psychological models of learning are applied to the development of material for communication-impaired children. There is an attempt to bridge the gap which often exists between psychological theory and educational practice.

The work reported in this chapter represents a view that providing enhanced opportunities for interaction not only influences quality of life and opportunities, but also provides us with insights into hidden cognitive abilities. In this sense, the technology becomes a tool for both the learner and for the teacher or researcher. For the learner, technology can be a tool for communicating thoughts, ideas, opinions, skills, etc. For the teacher or the researcher the technology can become an evaluation tool revealing the presence of hidden or trapped potential. Use of the technology in the manner described here provides additional evidence that we are often guilty of underestimating potential. The use of technology to empower individuals to demonstrate skills which would otherwise remain unexpressed has a relevance which extends beyond the immediate context of its use with the communication impaired. It addresses the nature of cognition in a technological society. The work described here can be placed in a context which again emphasizes the importance of applying a psychological component to the use of technology with disadvantaged groups. Out of such applications comes an appreciation that technology can be utilized to serve as an aid to cognitive expression and cognitive growth. Again '. . . what the mind can do depends upon the devices provided by the culture.' (Olson, 1976) but more significantly it depends on the intelligent use of those devices to serve as a means to achieve the goals of cognitive and personal growth.

8 Symbols of Thought

Writing and Word Processing

> The printing press had profound cognitive and social consequences, but its effect will not compare with the consequences of interactive information tools that function with the basic currency of human thought processes, the symbol.
>
> Pea (1985)

The significance of writing

Of all the symbols of human thought expressed via an 'enabling technology', perhaps the one with which we are most familiar is the written word, and modern technology has re-directed attention to the significance of writing via the development of ever more powerful and easy-to-use word-processing packages. It is virtually impossible to go into an elementary school today without being aware that young children are increasingly using word processors. The evidence is usually all around, displayed on classroom walls in the form of poems, stories and news-sheets all produced by some form of word-processing package. There is general agreement that using word processors appears to aid motivation – children are reported to write more, to be more motivated and to take an increased pride in their printed productions (Daiute, 1985). Writing with a computer is consider-ably easier than with a pen or pencil – words can be spaced evenly, erasure is straightforward and using the keys on a computer doesn't hurt your fingers as much as struggling to hold a pencil and form the letters. What is more, whatever you write inevitably looks good when it is printed, and appearance is often taken as indicative of quality! This is not just in the eyes of the writer, as Peacock (1988) has produced evidence which indicates that word-processed English language essays received higher grades than hand-written essays.

Practical significance of writing skills

Given the problems young children experience with conventional hand-writing it is hardly surprising that word processing is seen as a welcome relief. However, the ease of use of many of the word processing packages currently used in schools misses the point. In order to consider the real potential of word processing in the classroom, we need to ask first why we want children to develop good writing skills. After all, most of their communication is not via writing. Obviously, one argument is that for the foreseeable future, much of our educational evaluation will require that children are able to communicate with the written word. Further, the development of telecommunications and distance education will ensure that written communication of ideas, information and intentions will continue to be important. Already, there are schools whose computers are linked locally, nationally and internationally. International linkages, involving rapid satellite transmission, allow children living in varying cultures to communicate with each other, sharing very different experiences. Consider, for example, the problems faced by children in the United States and England trying to explain the rules of baseball and cricket respectively – a real problem in communication where differences in world knowledge can result in differences in interpretation and understanding. Such problems will be magnified where cultural experiences are even greater.

Communication in such cases is via the written word, and there may be very real challenges for those involved in the communication – challenges which involve the description of differences in lifestyle, environments and experiences. Such communications foster not merely an awareness of other cultures, but, given the medium of the communication, develop an awareness of the power and problems of text as a communication tool for conveying ideas and information.

The concept of the communicative power of the written word is an important one. In describing his 'Beach' microworld (see p. 111), Bob Lawler (1982) writes of his 3-year-old daughter

> . . . the learning of reading and the learning of writing have been synchronized (as speaking and interpreting speech are for the toddler); she learned to read her 30-word vocabulary by learning first to 'write', i.e., key the words on the computer terminal. Writing was an essential part of controlling the computer microworld that engaged her.

In this microworld, single typed words call up pre-defined Logo procedures. Typing the word 'sun' causes a picture of a sun to be drawn on the screen, the word 'car' causes a car to appear, etc. There is a relationship between the words used and the effects produced, together with a growing awareness that the written word can have a power of its own, that it can make interesting and personally significant things happen. The notion that the written word can take on this power, and can be used as an 'empowering tool' to help achieve personal targets and to make things happen is, to use Papert's terminology, a 'powerful idea'. It gives written language a functional significance which is often mainly associated with spoken language. John Cameron (personal communication) of the North York Board of Education in Toronto writes

> Students who have found writing an agonizing experience approach the word processor with interest and with confidence . . . [they] . . . are for the first time in their lives taking control, imposing their will on an electronic page. The experience may well change them very deeply.

Writing and cognition

There is a more fundamental aspect to the acquisition of good writing skills, one which relates to the development of cognition and to what writing makes possible. Writing is more than the external symbols of speech. Speech, by its very nature, is essentially temporary. By speaking, we can express ideas, share opinions, etc., but the processing limitations of human short-term memory mean that much of what we say and hear is lost. It is very difficult to recall, in detail, a conversation, and even more difficult to reflect on the implications of that conversation. In contrast, writing has a permanence which encourages reflectivity. We can re-read text; can pursue the lines of argument and consider the implications. We can read descriptive material at leisure, and imagine the scenes described by the author. It is this permanent quality of text that prompted Olson's argument that the development of a writing technology led to profound changes in human cultural and intellectual activities. An essential quality of written material is that we can stand back from the material, re-examine it, go away from it and come back to it. Of writing, Daniel Chandler (1984) states

Its very visibility invites, as it were, a mental magnifying glass, making it potentially a powerful tool of thought.

Writing, then, acts to enable reflective thinking – reflection both on one's own writing and on the writing of others. As long ago as 1933, John Dewey argued that reflective thought freed humans from impulsive and routine activity, and allowed us to act in a deliberate and intentional fashion. For Dewey, reflective thinking involves a linked sequence of ideas leading to a conclusion which can be substantiated by examining the environment or by studying one's own body of world knowledge. Dewey also outlined two phases of reflective thinking.

1. A state of doubt, hesitation and uncertainty in which thinking originates.
2. An act of searching to find the material which will resolve the uncertainty.

One can see here a parallel with Piaget's ideas of disequilibrium and accommodation, processes which Piaget conceived of as essential to cognitive growth. Moreover, we can see also how writing is involved as it enables the writer to express thoughts on paper, and to examine any discrepancies between what is written and what is intended.

Donald Graves (1983), a leading authority on the development of children's writing, takes this model further. He writes

Children grow as writers because they wrestle with imbalances between their intentions and the problems at hand. That is what growth is all about, being stretched, but not to the point where the problem encountered makes no sense at all. Writers are not aware of most of their problem solving since they relate closely to what they already can do.

Graves thus perceives the relationship between writing and cognitive accessibility. For reflective thought to mature, the children must accept intellectual responsibility, i.e., perceive the discrepancies and inconsistencies of their own thinking. This perspective again reflects Dewey's earlier views

When pupils study subjects that are too remote from their experience, that arouse no active curiosity, and that are beyond their power of understanding . . . they tend to become intellectually irresponsible; they do not ask for the meaning of what they learn, in the sense of what difference it makes to the rest of their beliefs and to their actions.

We thus have a perspective which envisages writing as being a tool in the development of metacognition. When children reflect on the nature of their writing, they are, in essence, utilizing a metacognitive skill – they are thinking about the implications of their own thinking. In dealing with writing children have to distinguish between what is intended and what is actually expressed in the written message. A growing awareness of potential inconsistencies and ambiguities reflects their develop- ing awareness of others' perspectives and points of view – i.e., their interpretation or intention may not be shared by others. The ability to take on the perspective of others; to consider other people's views and opinions as valid; to consider them as potentially valuable contributions to one's own cognitions are characteristics of mature thinking. Unfortunately, they are also abilities which remain elusive to many adults! Graves' writing methodology is designed to assist the child in this process. Beginning with the appropriate world knowledge, children are encouraged to express this knowledge and to develop it through research, restatement and re-examination. The child is guided by the teacher's questioning and by conferencing, which en- courage the young writer to reflect on what has been written. The child then goes back to the text, adds to it, reorganizes it and revises it before again meeting with the teacher for guidance. This is a cyclical process, in which the child is the initiator and the teacher provides supportive guidance. Its major purpose is to help children gain control of the writing process and thereby to establish a perspective on, and control over, their own thinking.

Writing is thus linked to cognition. Indeed, Sylvia Scribner

(1969) has argued that literacy is a necessary component in the development of abstract thinking. She argues that writing is a process by which internal propositions and statements are given an external form by writing and that the process of revision allows for the manipulation of these externalized ideas. The basis of her argument is that cognitive growth is enhanced where individuals can actively manipulate the materials that surround them, and that the revision of text incorporates such active manipulation. The text manipulation and revision possibilities provided by word processors offers a unique opportunity to examine such a hypothesis. Greenfield (1984) predicts that

. . . as writing by computer becomes more widespread it will lead to better performance by a larger proportion of the population on the type of formal problem solving involving the mental manipulation of abstract propositions.

The acquisition of writing skills thus goes beyond its use as a tool for communication. The effective use of this tool also involves the development and application of a range of cognitive skills. Here, 'effective use' does not just imply the learners' control of their own writing, but also their understanding of written text. Effective reading also demands the use of higher-order skills including comprehension monitoring, self-checking and sensitivity to reading goals – metacognitive skills which are also applicable to the development of good writing skills.

Role for word processing

Having hopefully established that the acquisition of writing skills remains of considerable significance in a technological society, is it not then sufficient simply to state that the use of word processors can make the task of writing easier? Clearly, using a word processor is often easier than writing with pen or pencil. Once you have even a very limited familiarity with the keyboard layout, something which young children acquire very rapidly, then the production of text becomes simple and rapid. Children as young as 5 or 6 will confidently enter text, using the 'magic eraser' (the delete key) and insert text in different places. Their sense of achievement and pleasure in their finished product is obvious, and a testament to the motivational potential of well-designed word processors. What constitutes a 'well-designed' word processor is addressed later, but in general terms implies that the tool is easy to use. Word processors which place several hurdles in the way of entering text, inserting extra text and generally manipulating text are likely to be de-motivating for novice users. A good word processor should encourage the creative use of text and be designed to facilitate text entry and text manipulation. However, this, in itself, is not enough. In order to appreciate fully the potential which is inherent in a good word processor, it is important to outline what constitutes a good writer, as this ultimately defines a sound educational word processor, and the extent to which word processors can foster the development of good writing skills, which serve both communication and cognitive growth.

Characteristics of good writers

A great deal of the relevant work on writing has been expertly summarized by Krashen (1984) in a short text entitled *Writing: Research, Theory and Applications*, and much of what follows on the characteristics of good writers is significantly influenced by that book. Krashen identifies a number of important compo-nents in examining what we know about learning to write. In brief, these concern the relationships between:

1. Reading and writing.
2. Writing and writing frequency.
3. Writing and instruction.
4. The composing process – planning, rescanning, revising, recursion and awareness of audience.

Relationships between reading and writing

The research indicates that voluntary pleasure reading contri-butes to the development of writing skills. A home influence exists in that homes of good writers have more books and parents tend to read more to good writers. 'Readers' show greater writing fluency and complexity. Exposure to a wide range of texts probably increases the child's awareness of differing styles of text. Studies have also compared groups who wrote frequently with those writing less but reading more. Findings indicate that the 'readers' produce better writing in terms of content, mechanics, organization, grammar and phrasing.

The question of the relationship between writing and writing frequency addresses the question of whether practice *per se* adds to ability. In general, better writers do more writing both in and outside school and writers do a greater variety of writing. Simply increasing school writing frequency does not seem to result in major gains.

Writing and instruction

Some aspects of writing skills can be taught, for example, form and organization. A more useful aspect of instruction is the feedback provided and the evidence indicates that this is useful when done between drafts, but is less useful when done at the end. Conferencing on specific features also helps. Contrary to many expectations, grammar instruction is not effective. Increasing reading at the expense of grammar is more effective.

Composing process

As would be predicted, good writers have better procedures for getting ideas onto paper. This involves several processes.

1. Planning – good writers plan more. This does not just mean producing a written plan. Good writers think more about both content and organization; have more flexible plans, and are more prepared to change ideas and to revise their draft.
2. Rescanning – good writers rescan more. This assists in maintaining a sense of the whole composition. Rescanning helps the writer review the overall plan, consider new ideas and incorporate changes.
3. Revision – good writers revise more. Better writers focus on content and less able writers on surface form. Advanced writers focus on content, often changing the meaning. Average writers concentrate on clarifying the meaning pre-

sent in the first draft, whereas poor writers focus on grammar and spelling.

4. Recursion – good writers may not adhere to an original plan or draft. They are prepared to revise their material, and the writing of a draft may be interrupted by more planning with recycling to earlier stages of the process.

5. Awareness of audience – good writers are more aware of the audience for whom they are writing, and take into account the likely interests and capabilities of that audience. Less able writers are not able to stand back and perceive their text from the perspective of another. This ability is not just a character- istic of a good writer, it is also a characteristic of more mature cognition.

In general, the work on the composing process indicates that it is not a smooth, linear process. There may be frequent revisions, involving alterations to original plans and schemes before a final version is produced. This fact often comes as a surprise to young writers who frequently believe that authors simply produce a perfect draft on their first attempt. Using the fact that many of their favourite authors (e.g., Roald Dahl) engage in this cyclical process can be a useful model in developing an awareness of the drafting and editing process.

The writing schema

Krashen's review provides a number of important guidelines concerning how to approach the development of good writing skills. Further, it is possible to distinguish between competence – what the writer knows about writing – and performance, the ability to put the knowledge into practice.

In terms of competence, good writers have a sound internal model of the writing process and have access to that knowledge. They have a more complex mental model or schema to call upon, which comes from increased reading of a variety of styles. Taking this model, the implication for the acquisition of writing skills is that writing ability is significantly enhanced via exten- sive reading where the reader's attention is on the message and not on the structure. A wide variety of reading will expose the reader to the necessary grammatical structures, increasing the probability that learners will incorporate these structures into their internal models. The complexity and subtlety of formal grammatical rules is such that instruction is only likely to succeed in teaching the most obvious aspects.

It should, however, be pointed out that reading is a necessary but not a sufficient condition for the acquisition of writing competence. Not all readers become good writers, and other factors which appear to be important include such motivational aspects as the learner's expectation of success at writing together with a desire both to write, and to write competently.

The other broad category that can be identified is that of performance. The underlying argument is that writing competence develops as a result of voluntary pleasure reading. The evidence which relates writing frequency to ability can be explained by stating that practice helps performance. It assists the writer in discovering an efficient composing process. The writer must, however, have an adequate internal model for this to occur. A potential value of instruction here is that it can assist in providing the writer with a model of the composing process, something which is not obvious from reading. Note, however, that having an adequate model of the composing process will not ensure good writing. The latter will come from exposure via reading, together with an application of the process of composition.

Implications of research

These are clear; if we want children to acquire good writing skills, then it is important that we emphasize reading for meaning and writing to convey meaning. To do this we need to provide an educational environment which assists the acquisition of those aspects. Too early an over-emphasis on the surface form of text (grammar, spelling, punctuation) is likely to be counter-productive and to reduce the motivation to write. Good writers appear to be good readers who have also acquired a knowledge of the process of writing. We should thus encourage the development of reading skills, including the metacognitive components associated with reading for meaning (monitoring, self-checking, identifying goals). It is also important that reading is not seen as a chore, but is encouraged as a worthwhile activity which can serve personal goals and interests. Further, it is important to help children develop an efficient composing process to assist them with their writing. Significant features in the composing process involve planning, revision (of both plan and text), rescanning to check on meaning and overall structure, and developing an awareness of the potential audience. Young writers need to be aware that writing is essentially a 'messy' process in which plans and drafts should be in a state of almost constant modification, and in which the surface aspects of grammar, spelling and punctuation are attended to at the later stages of the process.

Role of word processors

The introduction of word processors offers a new tool for assisting the acquisition of writing skills. What is important is to consider how that tool can be used in the light of what we know about such skills.

Perhaps one of the most obvious aspects about the acquisition of good writing skills is that handwriting does not appear to be an essential component in developing literacy. Indeed, the physical effort of handwriting can be seen as a potential hindrance. Anyone who has observed young children struggling to form letters or developing anxiety about untidy handwriting can attest to this fact. However, there is a more serious aspect to this. What can be termed 'the illegible penmanship crisis' can have negative motivational consequences for young children. Their awareness that handwriting is difficult, and that their own productions are, to their own eyes, inadequate can develop an attitude which perceives writing as a task to be avoided rather than one to be enjoyed for its potential creativity. For this reason, many have welcomed the advent of word processors, simply because they allow for easy entry and manipulation of text. The text entry facilities of modern word processors make writing physically and cognitively easier. Children no longer have to concentrate on letter formation, and are free to concentrate on the content rather than the form. Moreover, the printing capabilities mean that the printed output can match that of a conventionally published text. This, in itself, is an important motivational aspect, and many teachers report an increased interest in writing when done via the medium of a word processor in the classroom. This is a good beginning, but, on its own, is less than satisfactory. The fact that word processors make it easier to enter and change text does not, by itself, mean that writing will inevitably improve – more does not mean better.

There is a double-edged quality to word processing. As already mentioned, any standard word processor allows for the output of text to a printer. The text can often be modified by using different print styles and sizes, producing quite dramatic effects. No matter how it is printed, it invariably 'looks good'. This, quite reasonably, is often seen as a positive feature, particularly for young children. However, it is important to avoid the perfect-first-copy phenomenon. Novice writers tend to concentrate on the surface form of their writing, which includes its physical appearance. The danger here is that young writers will be satisfied by a first production because it looks neat when printed. Further, when revising text, novice writers tend to change the surface features first, to attend to spelling and to grammar without considering the meaning. The ease of text manipulation, and the presence of spelling checkers, although potentially advantageous, also contain possible disadvantages, in that having made such surface changes, the writer will once again be satisfied with the perfect-looking copy, produced at the push of a button. Word processors enable such surface changes to be made very easily and neatly, with a minimum of effort. However, the research findings summarized earlier indicate that an emphasis on such surface aspects of writing is unlikely to result in major gains in the acquisition of good writing skills.

The research on writing clearly indicates two dominant features – exposure to and experience of a wide range of styles via reading, together with an awareness of the writing process. If word processors are to fulfil their real potential in the classroom then they must lend themselves to applications which incorporate these aspects.

Reading–writing relationships

As indicated earlier, a close relationship exists between reading
and writing. Consequently, one of the first activities that a word
processor should support is that of reading. The public nature of
displaying text on a screen or of printing out good-quality copy
creates an awareness that material is to be read. Indeed, the
presence of text on screen can act as a powerful stimulus to
others to read and comment upon the material. This can often be
disconcerting for a novice writer, but can also help stimulate
awareness of others' views together with a growing sense of the
impact of the written material on the potential audience.
However, computer-mediated creative writing can be supported at a different level. So, for example, in a program like
'Story Maker' (developed at Bolt, Beranek and Newman)
children construct stories by selecting from a range of possible
options. This program presents a simple piece of text, and then
offers a set of alternative possibilities from which the child
chooses. Each choice leads to a range of further choices, and
when completed, the finished story can be copied onto a printer.
In one sense, such a program seems to be stretching the
conventional definition of a word processor, which usually
requires the entry of text by the user. In 'Story Maker' the text is
provided, and the child selects from the possibilities on offer.
However, 'Story Maker' contains important elements relevant
to the development of both reading and writing skills. The
structure is such that children have to think about the meaning
of the text and of the possible alternatives. They are thus reading
for meaning, but are also in a position of control in that they can
determine the direction the story takes, so that the final version
is essentially their creation. Should more structure be required,
children can elect to be given a goal at the beginning of the story.
In working towards the goal, once again children have to reflect
on the meaning of the text, but also have to make predictions,
evaluate and work towards a goal. In such activities, children are
exercising those metacognitive skills which are characteristic of
good readers, and are also gaining an awareness of a range of
skills relevant to good composition.

Stages in developing writing skills

A role for word processors at the early stages of writing is to support activities which are conducive to the development of good writing skills. The ease of text entry has already been referred to as a significant factor, as has the sense of control of entering letters and seeing them appear on the screen. Other programs allow children to enter words in order to create a picture on the screen, or to combine words in a short phrase to create a graphics effect. These are important activities, which promote a sense of awareness of the potential functional significance of writing. However, on their own, they are no guarantee that good writing skills will develop, although they can help create a positive attitude towards writing, something which may be difficult with conventional pencil/paper technology.

Good writing develops as a result of combining reading skills with an understanding and control of the process of writing. Although programs like 'Story Maker' can help highlight the relationships between composition and reading and possess a strong motivational appeal, word processors, on their own, are unlikely to result in major gains in reading skills. Other reading activities have a greater significance, particularly home-based voluntary reading. The major area where word processors can assist the development of good writing skills would seem to be in providing a young writer with control over the process of writing, and supporting the activity of composition. Graves (1979, 1983) reports that writers, whether experts or beginners, follow similar steps in composing – pre-writing, writing and revision. Word processors offer the potential to support each of these. This process can be further broken down to identify the particular steps a professional writer might go through in the production of a piece of material. There is a cyclical process involving the following activities:

plan, draft, read, re-draft, discuss, final copy, present, reflect

It is relatively easy to see how a word processor could support such a cycle of activities. Thus, the provision of a 'planner' within a word processor enables the writer to enter initial ideas, or for a teacher to suggest a possible outline. So, for example, in a child-centred word processor called 'PenDown' (published by Logotron, UK), an option called 'The Planner' offers a structured pre-writing facility. 'The Planner' operates at different levels, so that the initial plan can be extended and developed via the use of sub-headings which expand on the original themes. The plan can be called up at any time for examination, or additional material may be added to the plan. The development of pull-down windows and split-screen facilities clearly offer opportunities to develop such planning facilities, so that plans can be examined rapidly in the presence of current text, thereby facilitating an examination of the extent to which material is adhering to the initial plan, and enabling alterations to be made to the plan if required.

Word processors currently being used in schools offer a range of facilities designed to facilitate writing and to enhance its motivational aspects. In addition to such fairly standard features allowing for insertion, over-writing, deletion, manipulation, WYSIWYG (what you see is what you get), search, search and replace, text centring, spelling checkers, etc., additional features are often available which seem to be particularly suitable for school use. For very young children, large-size text can be displayed on the screen. A common feature which appears to be particularly appealing to children, is the availability of different print styles and page layouts, together with the option to combine different styles of print. Thus, some word processors come with such options as a 'newspaper' layout, enabling the printing of text in columns together with headlines and different print options. These provide a good opportunity for children to engage in collaborative writing to produce a class newspaper. Such an activity, apart from its motivational qualities, enhances awareness of audience, together with a developing sense that different styles of writing are appropriate to achieve various effects, again features of good writing and communication skills. The role of group work in collaborative writing stimulates a sharing of ideas and an increasing appreciation of the role of others in such a process. Another aspect which seems particularly relevant is the relatively simple feature of text manipulation. This enables a writer to mark sections of text and to move them to other parts of the composition. This can be used to encourage writers to reflect on the sequence of ideas used, and allows for an examination of the overall structure of text, and how its meaning and impact can be influenced by the order in which ideas are presented.

Word processors as empowering environments

Word processors are empowering environments in the sense defined by John Seely Brown (see p. 15). By the nature of the facilities they provide, they make many things possible which would otherwise be difficult. They also share the feature that the effects they can produce may result in an over-emphasis on performance rather than on the process, for example, by the perfect-first-copy phenomenon. Further, however, the range of facilities available on a word processor is such that it may overwhelm the novice user. Many features are inappropriate for early use, and may be confusing. Too much information can result in a loss of motivation and can be detrimental to learning. What would seem to be a more educationally sound course to take is to consider the characteristics of young writers as they move from novice to experienced writer, and to consider what features of word processors seem to be particularly relevant at each level. This is not to imply that other features could not be introduced if required, but it does provide an overall framework for a developmentally based introduction of word-processor-based writing activities.

The novice writer

The 'novice writer' is seen as initially concerned with mastering the symbol system of writing. A major advantage of a word processor at this stage is that it bypasses the laborious task of writing with a pencil and enables rapid and easy presentation of text on the screen. Although searching for the relevant letters on a keyboard takes time, children rapidly gain familiarity with such an activity, freeing their powers of concentration for the writing task rather than a letter-formation task. At this stage, a word processor for the beginning student should be simple, with a small number of commands, for example, insert, delete, save text, load text and print text. Its primary purpose is to provide the beginning writer with the opportunity to record thoughts and to make minor corrections. Entry of text should be straightforward, not requiring any advance specification of page or text layout. A useful analogy at this stage is that of a notebook in which text can be entered at any time, with minimum attention given to conventions of style. If text entry is to be simple, insertion of additional text should also be simple. The writer should be able to go to the point at which new text is to be placed and be able to start writing, without any need to specify in advance how many words are to be entered or how much space is to be made. Equally with deleting text, children are familiar with the notion of a 'magic eraser', and with the idea that a cursor can be moved to the desired point and text removed. A cautionary note here, is that a form of 'safety net' should be provided, so that if text is deleted it is not irretrievably lost. The notion of a 'bin' into which deleted text is placed is a useful one, coupled with the idea that text can be brought out of the bin for re-examination. The fact that material cannot be lost accidentally, together with the opportunity a bin system provides for examining different possibilities, also has the advantage that it helps create an awareness in the writer's mind that change is possible. It also gives the writer the opportunity to examine different ways of expressing the same idea.

A further feature particularly relevant for young writers is the opportunity to combine text with a drawing facility. Young children enjoy drawing, and their pictures invariably tell a story. The opportunity to combine pictures and words not only adds to the motivational aspects, but imbues writing with a functional significance that can be readily understood by the child.

The saving and loading of text should also be straightforward, with built-in safety features to reduce the possibility of children loading text when they meant to save it and vice versa. Having produced text on the screen, it is crucially important that the child can obtain a 'hard copy' in the form of a printed version. At this level, printing should support different styles of print – a particular favourite with young children seems to be 'jumbo' size print. Although many word processors support a wide variety of print options, it would seem inappropriate to expose young children to the full range.

The intermediate writer

By the time children have mastered the above commands and features, they have essentially 'cracked' the code of writing, as well as having gained a good basic idea of what a word processor makes possible. At this point, their command of writing is such that increasing attention can be given to the process of writing.

The ease of text entry which was a major advantage for the novice writer is no longer a major feature, particularly if children have not acquired some degree of keyboarding skills at this point. If the child is more familiar with using pen and paper than with using a computer keyboard, the introduction of a word processor may increase cognitive load, resulting in a deterioration of the student's writing quality. Notwithstanding this possibility, word processors still offer major advantages to the intermediate writer, although there may be a period when it is necessary for students to acquire keyboard familiarity if they had not been using word processors during the earlier stage of learning to write.

By this time, the level of linguistic competence is such that the average child should be aware of the presence of sentences and paragraphs. This makes it possible for rapid movement through the text according to linguistic units. Obviously, the option to move less rapidly, word by word or line by line is still present, but the facility to move sentence by sentence or paragraph by paragraph adds to the ease with which text can be scanned, and new text inserted or old text deleted. In addition, a 'search and replace' option is probably appropriate at this level, to speed up corrections.

As the novice writer begins to master the code of writing and progresses to the stage of 'intermediate writer', additional features may become relevant. So, for example, it may be appropriate to use a simple spelling checker or dictionary. The latter can be particularly useful when combined with a thesaurus and the option for the children to enter their own words, thereby creating their own dictionaries and word banks, which could be arranged alphabetically or by theme. The facility to create a dictionary or a thesaurus gives the student a considerable degree of independence, and can also be used to support a range of associated study skills. So, for example, students could create their own dictionaries associated with a particular topic area they were covering in class. Setting up such a dictionary requires the use of additional information skills in order to discover what to enter into the dictionary and how the information should be organized.

In carrying out the above activities, students are increasingly involved in planning, and the introduction of a word-processor-based planner is appropriate at this level. The planning facility described earlier enables students to produce a basic plan which can be extended through headings and subheadings, and to which new ideas can be added. In producing and modifying a plan, writers are increasingly reflecting on the intentions of their composition. Producing a plan encourages students to consider relevant information and how it should be incorporated into their text, thus drawing attention to the importance of the structure of the text and the organization of ideas.

By this stage, the intermediate writer is becoming aware of writing as a process to communicate ideas and images. This communication process can be enhanced by the provision of a broader range of formatting and printing options than is required for the beginning writer. Opportunity to indent and centre text, and to use a wider range of print options adds to the motivational appeal, and can be used to good effect to create special effects. By using such options, students have to think about the type of effect they wish their printed text to create, developing their awareness of audience.

At this stage, there is an increased emphasis on the process of writing rather than on the basic transcription of ideas onto paper or the screen. The facilities most appropriate to an intermediate writer increasingly enable the writer to modify the text and to structure it to accomplish particular goals. The features which made word processing particularly suitable for beginning writers remain relevant to intermediate writers, but are of less significance in comparison with those activities which support the cognitive aspects of good writing, for example, planning and revision. As students gain control of these processes, they shift from being 'intermediate' writers to becoming 'advanced writers'.

Advanced writers

All those facilities which supported the beginning and intermediate writers can also assist the advanced writer. However, what differentiates the advanced writer from the earlier stages is the degree of control exercised over the writing process. An advanced writer is able to move easily between the different levels involved in writing. The surface features of grammar and syntax have, to a large extent, been mastered, and cognitive attention is concentrated on the process of writing. Advanced writers make particular use of planning and revision. The revision, however, does not just involve correction of spelling and grammar. High level revision requires revision of ideas, and an examination of both text and plan to ensure that the intended message is conveyed. An advanced writer is aware that different styles can be used to create different effects, and that effective communication demands an awareness of audience. In essence, advanced writers are initially more concerned about the coherence of their text, its impact and audience appeal than they are about its technical correctness.

Certain word processor facilities are particularly suitable at this stage of the writing process. Of particular significance are operations which assist movement around the text and movement of the text. 'Cut and paste' operations (i.e., where a segment of text can be marked and moved to another place) should be especially flexible and simple to use as advanced writers will use such options to reorganize material. (Note that writers at an earlier stage may also find a 'cut and paste' option useful.) At this level, writers should also be able to call up for preview as much of their composition as possible, in order to be able to read through what they have already written. Also useful here are windows and pull-down and split-screens which can simultaneously display plans and scroll text.

Ideas processors

Of considerable potential for advanced writers are recent advances in the field of word processing which assist with the structuring of ideas and material. These can be seen as advanced planners which simplify the creation and manipulation of outlines. These programs deal more with the organization of text than with writing it. So, for example, a Xerox product called 'Notecards' enables text to be organized into almost any kind of structure. The organization can be done prior to writing or after the fact, and allows the writer to enter notes of any length or type which can then be linked to other entries in the system. The links can also be labelled, and retrieval facilities enable the collection of all entries having certain descriptions or connected by certain links. The provision of such programs not only makes possible the development of very flexible plans and outlines, but also enables the writer to organize material in a variety of ways, and to examine the links which exist between differing entries in the system. Such a facility offers the opportunity to examine one's own thinking, and to reflect on and perceive relationships which otherwise might have been forgotten or overlooked. Such tools represent a considerable advance on conventional planners which often require an author to specify an outline and then to modify that existing plan. What is required are tools which help in the process of modifying the plan, not just modifying the text. Ideas processors like 'Notecard' represent a step in this direction. They can be perceived as a form of electronic note-pad on which ideas, notes, tentative thoughts, and possibilities can be entered without the author having to use cognitive resources in thinking about where they belong in a formal plan. John Seely Brown refers to such systems as being like '. . . a fishnet, catching and supporting ideas without demanding that they be in some prespecified form' and argues that such systems provide an environment which '. . . enhances the process of writing, that helps an author move from prearticulate intuitions to articulate arguments, from chaos to order in thinking and writing'.

Conclusion

It is appropriate to end this chapter with another quotation from John Seely Brown. Word processors are potentially empowering environments in the sense defined by him. They make certain tasks easier, and they contain the potential to help develop the process of writing as well as the product. Used appropriately, they can help encourage reflection on the writing process, and bring children to an awareness that they can be members of 'the writers' club'. However, the potential power of word processors is such that their introduction into the classroom needs to be approached with caution. The development of writing skills is such that different facilities are more appropriate at different points, according to whether the writer is at a beginning, intermediate or advanced stage. Word processors will only be empowering in the sense that they can respond to and support the needs, abilities and characteristics of children at different stages in this process. Word processors are a cognitive tool in all senses. They have the potential to reify (make concrete) our cognitions in ways unequalled by any other writing technology, but the on-screen reflections of our thoughts remain malleable. We can examine and explore our implications and intentions, and play with our thoughts as we played with the building bricks of our childhood. Words on the screen are the symbols of our cognitions, but unlike words on paper they remain flexible – we can mould them until their message matches our intentions. At that point they will indeed reflect our thoughts, and, if we consider their meaning, we will reflect on the nature of our own cognition, thereby gaining a greater insight into, and control over, our own thinking.

9 Intelligent Tutoring Systems in Education

Introduction

Running through the issues addressed so far are two inter-related themes. The first is that one role computers can play in education is a cognitive one, assisting the development and expression of a range of cognitive skills. Less explicitly stated is the theme that in order to achieve cognitive gains in the users, software should incorporate a certain degree of 'intelligence' in the sense that it is appropriate for particular target users and can assist them to formulate and to attain their objectives.

These aspects come together more specifically in the area of intelligent tutoring systems (ITSs) which aim to instruct learners in specific skills and subject areas. They also seek to be diagnostic and adaptive to pupils' individual behaviours in order to identify misconceptions so that instruction and remediation can take place. There are many thousands of such systems in operation daily throughout the world. They incorporate detailed knowledge of subject areas, of the students and of how to teach. They respond adaptively to individual differences in motivation and learning styles. They are aware of individual students' background knowledge and experiences. They can detect shifts in student attention and modify their teaching strategies in response to learner reactions. They call upon an extensive knowledge base in order to present the learning material; they present individualized feedback in order to facilitate learning, and are sensitive to individual differences in how students think. We have a term for such intelligent tutoring systems – good teachers.

What is it that distinguishes good teachers from the rest? Everyone has experienced good, bad and indifferent teachers. The good teachers are recalled with admiration, affection and (occasionally) a little trepidation. In general, research has indicated that factors like intelligence and personality are less important than the skills teachers use in the classroom environment. Good teachers facilitate student thinking, manage classrooms effectively, deliver high-quality instruction, evaluate learning and adapt to changing situations. In order to do this, they have to call upon a wide repertoire of skills. To foster thinking, they must understand something about the nature and limitations of human cognition. They must be able to make new information meaningful to novice learners, which implies that they must know something about the current state of understanding of those learners. Good teachers are not just aware of individual differences in intelligence, but are also aware that changes occur across time. The thinking style of an average 6-year-old is very different from that of a 10-year-old, which, in turn is different from that of a 15-year-old. Further, differences exist in cognitive style, which relates to the way learners perceive and deal with information. Cognitive style may not just vary between individuals, but may also change with time, competence and subject matter.

Good teaching, however, involves considerably more than just (!) responding to and enhancing cognitive abilities. It requires that attention be paid to motivational issues to enhance self-esteem and confidence, so that a positive attitude to learning is fostered. In order to achieve this, good teachers seek ways to help students satisfy personal goals, and use learner interests as an integral part of the educational process.

In terms of delivering instruction, effective teachers are aware of individual differences and plan and modify their material accordingly. They communicate clear goals and objectives which are attainable by the students. The best teachers provide learning environments in which all students are challenged because materials are suitable to their varying capabilities and interests. Having delivered good instruction, effective teachers evaluate learning, not just to monitor student learning and provide appropriate intervention and guidance, but also to assess their own performance. Instruction is carefully evaluated and adjusted. A human teacher is constantly updating the 'database' about the subject matter, the pupils, and about the most effective way of presenting information to those pupils.

Requirements for a machine-based 'intelligent tutor'

The above is not meant to belittle the advances made by the AI community in seeking to create intelligent computer tutors, but is intended to indicate the magnitude of the task. Various grandiose claims have been made for the potential of computer-based tutors, but it is probably reasonable to state that no machine-based 'intelligent tutor' has yet approached the degree of teaching expertise demonstrated by the average classroom teacher. However, progress has been made, and it is worth considering the nature of computer-based intelligent tutors, as they illustrate the enormity of the challenge.

The challenge which many researchers in the field of artificial intelligence have set themselves is the development of computerized teaching systems which seek to mimic some capabilities of human tutors. The aim is not (yet) to mimic the full performance range of a skilled human teacher, but to enhance a selected component of the teaching/learning interaction involving learner and computer. They attempt to do this by utilizing more advanced functions than earlier CAL systems – the ability to analyse individual student responses to detect patterns of errors, together with the ability to interact with the student by providing advice, guidance and by responding to student queries. These diagnostic, remedial and interactive aspects perhaps encapsulate the basic nature of an ITS, and distinguish such systems from earlier computer-mediated educational systems which presented a series of pre-defined problems for solution, together with a limited number of routes through the learning material.

The 'intelligence' of an ITS thus resides in its ability to respond adaptively to differing student inputs. In order to achieve this, an ITS requires certain components, specified by Hartley and Sleeman (1973):

1. Knowledge of the domain (subject matter).
2. Knowledge of the student (student model).
3. Knowledge of relevant teaching strategies.
4. Knowledge of how to apply the knowledge of teaching strategies to the needs of the individual (instructional model).

Other components seen as important include:

5. Presence within the system of an intelligent 'coach' or advisor.
6. Addition of intelligent 'help' facilities.
7. A natural language-understanding capability so that a dialogue can take place between the learner and the system.
8. The provision of a learning environment so that the learner can learn by doing.
9. The use of knowledge of individual learner's progress so that tuition can be individualized.

Assuming for the moment that such knowledge is readily available and that it can be specified in a sufficiently precise form to be encoded in a computer program then the cycle of operations of an intelligent teaching system is something like this (after Ross, 1987):

1. The system presents a problem.
2. The user makes a response.
3. The system produces analyses of the response using its 'knowledge' of the subject, the problem, the user and the user's past performance.
4. The system seeks confirmation of its analyses by further questioning of the student – this may illustrate the nature of the student's level of understanding.
5. The system decides what to do next using the information gained from its analysis and interactions with the student – this may lead to remediation if the student's responses have revealed areas of difficulty or misunderstanding. Remedial intervention can involve such things as a dialogue about the problem and the student's responses; examples which clearly illustrate the student's errors, or a breakdown of the problem so that the student concentrates on the diagnosed areas of weakness.

Procedural knowledge in simple arithmetic

Of the areas which have been addressed by intelligent tutoring systems, one of the best known, and most relevant to elementary education, is that of simple arithmetic involving the four rules of number. A major impetus here was that the research into the acquisition of arithmetic skills has a long history, and has significantly influenced previous attempts to automatize learning. Thus, Thorndike's work in the 1920s can be seen as an early attempt to provide a carefully structured approach to the learning of basic arithmetic, based on drill-and-practice principles. The development of technology has seen a continuation of this approach (e.g., Texas Instruments 'Little Professor'), and many arithmetic programs running on school computers fall into this paradigm. As indicated earlier there are occasions when a drill approach to arithmetic is appropriate (rehearsal of previously acquired skills, development of automaticity). However, such an approach does not reflect the advances which have been made in our understanding of the procedures or operations a learner uses when carrying out a calculation.

When presented with a subtraction problem like $623 - 457$, a learner needs to know what procedure to use to produce the correct answer. Application of the correct procedures in the above problem will generate the correct answer. Those with expertise at such three-column subtraction will probably be unaware of the various processes they utilize to solve such a problem. However, detailed analyses (protocols) of students carrying out such calculations have highlighted the steps involved and have helped throw light on the nature of possible errors.

Mayer (1981) lists the processes and decisions which are involved in solving problems like the one given above.

1. First you have to recognize the problem, identifying which digits belong in the units, tens and hundreds columns and whether they are in the top or bottom row. Having set up the problem, it has to be identified as a subtraction problem (rather than addition, for example), and that you will start at the right, in the units column.

2. Begin subtraction procedure. This consists of the following.
   (a) find $T - B$ (where T is a number on the top row and B is a number on the bottom row), for the column you are working on;
   (b) is $T < B$? If the top number is less than the bottom number, you need to use the borrow procedure in step 3. Otherwise, go on to 2(c);
   (c) subtract and write down the answer in the appropriate space for the current column;
   (d) continue – if there are more columns to the left, repeat the subtraction procedure, starting at 2(a). If there are no more columns, then stop.
3. Borrow procedure. Use this only if it is necessary to borrow (2(b)):
   (a) find the next T. Check the top number in the column to the left of the one you are working on to see if it is possible to borrow;
   (b) is next $T = 0$? If it is zero, then as it is not possible to borrow from zero use the 'borrow from zero procedure' in step 4;
   (c) add 10 to top number in the current column;
   (d) subtract 1 from the top number in the next left column.
   (e) go to step 2.
4. Borrow from zero procedure. This procedure is only used when there is a need to subtract from zero.
   (a) find next T which will be two columns to the left of the one currently being worked on;
   (b) is next $T = 0$? If it is, go on to some new procedure, otherwise continue;
   (c) subtract 1 from the top number in the second left column;
   (d) add 9 to top number in left column;
   (e) add 10 to top number in current column;
   (f) go to step 2.

This description of Mayer's may seem unnecessarily complex, but it documents in detail the procedures used when carrying out a multi-column subtraction problem. Note that it is assumed that the student can carry out basic subtraction of a one-column nature, and that the student can identify hundreds, tens and units, in order to set up the problem. Setting aside the fact that use of the procedure does not teach place value and that the widespread use of calculators in schools and society may arguably make redundant the acquisition of skills like column subtraction, the detailed description of the processes involved has certain advantages.

Infestations of arithmetic bugs

The most significant feature is that such a procedural analysis assists in the identification of particular types of student error. Suppose, for example, that a student gave the following answers

369	655	435	256	743
−235	−371	−221	−167	−352
134	324	214	111	411

One not very satisfactory way of proceeding here would be simply to indicate that some of the answers were incorrect and others correct, and ask the student to repeat those that were incorrect – a drill-and-practice methodology. However, there is a consistent *procedural* error in the above which enables the student to get some answers correct and others wrong. It is the common error of always subtracting the smaller number from the larger, irrespective of whether the number is at the top or bottom of the column. What we can say is that the student has a procedural error or 'bug' – which is very different from concluding that the student cannot subtract. Students' patterns of errors appear to reflect fundamental misunderstandings of procedures, rather than random errors in carrying out basically correct procedures. Where errors appear in a consistent pattern, this may be indicative of a misunderstanding of the steps involved in a procedure. In terms of describing the student's competence at arithmetic it may be more useful to describe what procedural knowledge a student has, rather than simply stating an end score. An examination of errors can help identify the way in which a student represents the problem in memory, even when it is represented in an incorrect way. The argument is not that the students do not possess procedures, nor that they cannot follow procedures, but that the procedures they have may be faulty or incomplete or incorrectly applied. The specification of a student's procedural knowledge allows for the identification of particular bugs which can then provide the basis for remediation directed at eliminating those bugs.

Brown and Burton (1978) have specified some of the common bugs which infect children's procedural knowledge for 3-digit subtraction. Amongst the most common are (adapted from Mayer, 1983)

1. Borrowing from zero – when borrowing from a top column with a top digit of zero, the student enters 9 in the column to the left of the one being worked on, but fails to continue borrowing from the column to the left of zero. $(704 - 306 = 498)$.
2. Smaller from larger – the student subtracts the smaller digit from the larger regardless of which one is on top. $(354 - 278 = 124)$.
3. Zero minus a number equals the number – whenever the top digit is zero the student enters the bottom digit as the answer. $(170 - 121 = 51)$.
4. Move over zero, borrow – when there is a need to borrow from a column whose top digit is zero, the student skips that column and borrows from the next one. $(304 - 75 = 139)$.
5. Zero minus a number equals the number and move over zero, borrow – whenever the top digit in a column is zero, the student enters the bottom number as the answer. When the student needs to borrow from a column with a top digit of zero, that column is skipped and the student borrows from the next column. $(304 - 75 = 179)$.

ITS for arithmetic

A further advantage of being able to specify precisely the steps involved in solving a problem is that it then becomes possible to create a computer program which can carry out those steps and which can identify when a user is not following the correct procedures, i.e., when individual bugs or combinations of bugs are present.

Burton and Brown (1979) used such procedural knowledge to

produce the ITS 'Buggy', probably the most cited example in the literature. They used this program to analyse the answers 1325 primary-school children gave to a set of 15 subtraction problems. If the answers were correct, Buggy categorised the student as using the correct algorithm. If, however, there were errors, Buggy attempted to find one bug which accounted for most or all of the errors. If no single bug could be found, various combinations were tried until the most suitable combination was identified. The program would thus search for many possible bugs and combinations of bugs (Brown and Burton claim 330 bugs for subtraction), and was able to identify the subtraction procedure used for about half the students. Buggy has also been used with trainee teachers to help them interpret a child's performance in terms of the routines which lead to a faulty performance. Buggy can thus be used to simulate a 'buggy' student and the task for the teacher is to discover and describe the bug.

A major advantage of a system like Buggy is that it can help develop the realization that apparently random errors may be the reflection of an underlying consistency. O'Shea and Self (1983) write

The realization that errors that appear random are the manifestations of systematic bugs is a breakthrough for many student teachers, and all those involved in the Buggy game felt they gained something valuable.

Buggy bugs

Although the approach adopted by Brown and Burton represents a significant advance on previous computer-based arithmetic packages, it is not without its problems. Nicolson (1988) lists a number of drawbacks, amongst which are:

1. The system is essentially diagnostic rather than remedial. In other words, it is good at identifying bugs, but not at specifying what to do about the errors. Many would probably conclude that it is easy enough to detect certain common bugs, but rather less easy to know how to correct them.
2. Brown and Burton list over 300 bugs for subtraction. It is difficult to envisage how the classroom teacher would be able

to deal with so many possible errors, either in terms of understanding what the bug meant or in terms of knowing what to do about it. This, of course, could reinforce the importance of a machine-based tutor, always assuming that this incorporated adequate knowledge of how to deal with errors.

3. In order to identify consistent bugs, it is necessary for the system to present a number of problems, thereby making immediacy of feedback difficult. Nicolson writes that Brown and Burton 'sacrificed their birthright' by forfeiting one of CAL's major advantages – the potential to provide immediate feedback.

4. Not all bugs are consistent – they may appear, disappear and change during the course of a session and between sessions.

The concept of bugs is a central one to any ITS. The basic philosophy is that a learner's errors relate to that learner's internal model of a task, and that certain errors will be sufficiently consistent both within and across learners to enable accurate diagnosis of particular misconceptions. There is, however, an additional complexity here which is that the nature of errors may change over time and expertise – experts and novices frequently have different knowledge and a different organization of knowledge. Not only that, but an individual student's knowledge and its organization (in schemata and in semantic networks) can vary greatly. Research in developmental and cognitive psychology has indicated the extent to which what is being learnt at any one particular time is greatly influenced by the preconceptions and knowledge structures learners bring to the situation. What this effectively implies is that individual students may well utilize different learning strategies.

Sleeman (1987) reports that a system which was able to diagnose the majority of difficulties encountered by 15-year-old algebra students was not able to diagnose errors made by 14-year-old students. He further argues that an individual's current state of knowledge results in that individual making inferences concerning how to tackle a new problem, and that the student may infer several rules which are consistent with a particular example, but which may be incorrect when applied more widely. This would imply that considerable individual variation may be present in determining which bugs are shown. Sleeman summarizes his argument by stating that

. . . the individual's initial knowledge profoundly influences the knowledge which is subsequently inferred, and captures the sense in which learners are active theory builders trying to find patterns, making sense out of observations, forming hypotheses, and testing them out.

This, however, is not to state that certain consistencies will not be present. So, for example, in the subtraction problems, many would recognize that students often show similar difficulties, for example, subtracting the smaller number from the larger, difficulties in borrowing, etc. Whether one needs a computer-based ITS to detect such common errors is another matter! Most of the teachers to whom I have shown examples of the most common subtraction bugs have quickly identified them. The problem seems to lie more in knowing what to do about them, not in detecting them!

ITS criticisms

Of course, in order to identify the existence of bugs, it is necessary to establish a catalogue of bugs, and to do this it would seem to be important to carry out detailed and lengthy investigations of humans actually solving problems. Sleeman (1987) argues strongly that such protocol analyses are essential if satisfactory bug catalogues are to be established in order to guide the development of diagnostic systems. Although this appears to be a relatively non-contentious proposal, Rosenberg (1987) reports that few ITS projects have actually incorporated detailed protocol analysis, pointing out that ITS implementors need to spend considerable time with both students and teachers in order to develop effective diagnostic models. Indeed, Rosenberg offers a wide ranging criticism of current ITS implementations. These criticisms, based on a review of work reported in both the education and computing literature, fall into two broad classes. In the first instance, it is argued that many implementations are not based in a model of learning, being more motivated by the available technology than by educational needs, and that ITS implementors rarely refer to work in education which could help guide their implementations. Rosenberg's second major area of criticism concerns the claims made for the effectiveness of ITS projects, which are often based on '. . . testing that is poorly controlled, incompletely reported, inconclusive, and in some cases totally lacking'.

Rosenberg argues that an adequate model of tutoring (essential if one is to develop an ITS) will not be achieved by listing error types nor by producing a computer-based representation of knowledge, although these may be important steps in the evolution of an ITS. What is required are systems which can respond to individual differences, and which do not implicitly incorporate a single particular model of learning. It would be ironic if those technological developments which have made genuine individualization possible were used to maintain the limited route-learning techniques of the old programmed learning systems.

The complexity of the task

The criticisms offered in part stem from the complexity of the task involved, i.e., to develop systems which mimic some of the capabilities possessed by human tutors. In seeking to achieve this within an educational context, ITS developers have inevitably been forced into restricted knowledge domains, where it is far easier to specify precisely the knowledge to be imparted (ITSs typically address narrow knowledge areas, for this reason). However, within a modern educational context, much of the knowledge we wish children to acquire is neither restricted nor domain specific. In an era when there is an increasing emphasis on the development and acquisition of broadly based information, scientific and metacognitive skills, one can again raise the question of whether there is much point in developing an ITS to teach basic arithmetic skills when all children are likely to have access to very low-cost calculators. In a related context, John Self (1985) writes

It is somewhat contradictory to imagine that expert systems will be developed to perform certain tasks, thereby rendering that area of human expertise redundant, and will then be used to teach that expertise.

In a paper entitled 'Bread today, jam tomorrow: the impact of AI on education', du Boulay and Sloman (1988) write

. . . good research in AI characteristically reveals problems that transform optimists into doubters, and there is at least as much reason for this to happen in the field of ITS as in work on vision, language understanding, learning and so on.

ITS requirements

To recap on the requirements for an ITS – an effective system will include knowledge of the domain, knowledge of the subject, knowledge of available teaching strategies and knowledge of how to apply those strategies to the needs of the individual. In general, the systems developed to date have concentrated on the first of these requirements – the representation of knowledge. Work in the field has clearly indicated that it is possible to represent knowledge sufficiently precisely for it to be encoded within software. In addition to basic arithmetic, ITSs have addressed such topics as BASIC programming, medical diagnosis, automotive electrics, probability theory, electronic trouble shooting, simple German syntax and the British Highway Code. What all these have in common is that they are well-defined knowledge areas, where the knowledge to be acquired can be readily specified. The problem does not lie in the question of whether it is possible to specify knowledge – it clearly is possible, and advances in cognitive science over the next few years will probably extend the range of areas where such precision is possible. The problem lies in producing ITSs which satisfy the remaining requirements – user model, teaching model and a model of the interactions between user and teaching strategy.

Predominant methodology

In general, the dominant methodology to date has been to concentrate on the expertise and to pay rather less attention to what learners actually think, do and know. In other words, most, if not all, ITSs are strong on their model of the subject matter but weak on their model of the user. The model of the user/learner which is usually incorporated is that the learner is an 'errorful expert', and that the goal of the system is to bring the learner to the state of knowledge as specified by the model of expertise incorporated in the system. In order to transfer knowledge or understanding, it is clearly necessary to have knowledge of the subject matter together with a model of the learner. However, the prevailing methodology in ITSs is such that little attention is given to what the learner brings to the situation, apart from a comparison between the learner's current state of knowledge in the required subject area in contrast with the desired state of knowledge as specified by the system. Clancy (1984) states that 'The model of the student's knowledge, as built by the program, is a subset of the idealized knowledge base.'

Real learners in real situations

Although this is a practical, hierarchical, structured, sequential goal-orientated course of action, it unfortunately does not reflect the way real learners learn in real situations. A vast body of research in developmental and cognitive psychology has indicated that an individual's learning is significantly influenced by prior knowledge, interpretations, expectations and motivations. Such work has revealed the presence of considerable individual differences in learning styles, which can shift across and within subject matter as learners move from novice to expert. So, for example, Turkle (1984) reports that amongst children using computers to learn simple programming, there were clear differences in learning style. Most teachers are aware that multiple styles exist and often try to react accordingly. There is little evidence to date that ITSs have approached such a level of sophistication. Perhaps more regrettably, there is little evidence to suggest that many ITS implementors are aware of relevant research which might help guide the development of more interactive and responsive systems.

Alternative approaches

Although the term ITS is widely used, it is perhaps an unfortunate one in that it emphasizes a tutoring style in which the system teaches the learner. Alternative approaches empha-size a shift in emphasis towards more exploratory styles of intelligent systems. In these scenarios (currently under develop-ment for a number of industrial training situations), a range of interactions is possible, for example:

1. The system sets up a problem.
2. The learner tries to solve the problem whilst receiving guidance from an intelligent coach within the system.
3. The learner is free to take the initiative and try new possibilities, observe consequences and receive comments from the coach.
4. The coach (within the system) can give the learner a 'guided tour' of a problem domain.
5. The coach can present a problem to solve and can offer guidance if requested.

Within such a situation, the aim is to give the learner a good conceptual understanding of the target domain rather than to impart knowledge *per se*. Such an approach offers the potential to give learners a good mental model of a knowledge domain, resulting in the development of more flexible and adaptable levels of understanding (Cumming, 1988).

Notice also that in such a situation the 'intelligent coach' acts as a guide and advisor. There are parallels here with Vygotsky's notions of a teacher acting as a facilitator to guide a learner through the zone of proximal development.

Learner-centred perspective

John Self (1985) has argued that the dominant philosophy guiding the development of 'intelligent' computer-assisted learning is, in fact, mistaken and that a major shift of emphasis should occur. The shift would be away from knowledge specification towards a learner-orientated approach. Thus,

. . . instead of treating student inputs as manifestations of errors to be eliminated, an alternative philosophy could emphasize the learner's present ability. The basic teaching strategy then would be to seek to extend this knowledge, but not necessarily towards some idealized goal (remembering that there is rarely a unique, 'correct' way to do anything significant).

Self is proposing a radically different approach to ITS development, one which adopts a learner-centred perspective on intelligent CAL. He envisages programs which reflect and adapt to the changes which occur in a learner during interaction with the learning material. Using such a perspective, Self speculates on a system that can access a large body of facts, but which does not have rigid rules for organizing these facts. The learner's role is to explore this database by asking questions and forming and testing hypotheses. In so doing, the learner will start to create a conceptual understanding of the material and, although the data is initially unstructured, will impose a structure upon it in order better to understand and integrate new information (humans try to impose meaning on new information, i.e., relate it to what they know and understand). The learner's initial state of knowledge or understanding will influence the manner in which exploration takes place and the nature of the mental models established. In Self's envisaged system, the learner's learning will be modelled by a machine-learning program which will use the same data accessed by the learner, and will generate its own model of the learner's state of understanding. The 'intelligence' or 'expertise' of the machine-learning system would not lie in the subject domain but in the interactions between the learner and the system. In order to build a model of the learner's model, the system would incorporate 'meta-rules' enabling it to ask questions, request information, provide prompts and encourage the learner to reflect on the nature of the material learnt.

In this sense, Self is asking for a computer implementation of human learning. Although this is likely to be a complex task (no-one ever claimed that human learning was simple!) research on machine learning, combined with developments in cognitive science, suggest that the attainment of such a goal would go a considerable way towards establishing adequate learner models within an ITS.

A further inherent advantage to the learner-centred perspective, is that attention would also be shifted towards the nature of successful tutoring. In general, three basic levels of guidance can be identified in instruction.

1. *Pure discovery* The learner receives minimal guidance, and is left to discover general principles with minimum intervention and support.

2. *Guided discovery*　The student is given problems to solve, but the instructor provides hints about how to solve those problems.
3. *Expository*　The final answer and rules are given to the learner.

Although pure discovery learning has an intuitive appeal, the realities of time, classroom management and individual differences mean that some learners will not be able to discover the appropriate concepts and rules without teacher intervention. At the other extreme, expository methods can reduce learning time, but do not ensure that the learner is cognitively engaged in processing the learning material. In general, when the goal is long-term retention and adequate coverage of subject matter, guided methods are superior, as they encourage learners to search actively for general rules and principles, and ensure that the learner is exposed to the desired material. In terms of ITSs, guided discovery methods appear to be favoured, which accords with research into the effectiveness of the differing paradigms. However, the success of guided discovery depends greatly on the ability of the teacher to identify when to intervene, how to provide guidance and what guidance to provide – an 'intelligent' tutor will need to incorporate a model to deal with these aspects.

Conclusion

If we consider what it is that good human tutors do, it is clear that they do more than make listings of errors (although it is equally clear that they are aware of error types). Successful tutoring has as much to do with human interaction as with identifying and correcting errors. A human tutor can teach simply by listening to a student describe a problem, for in describing the problem the student reflects more deeply on the thinking and may attain the solution without any 'apparent' assistance. On other occasions, the provision of supportive comments, gestures (a smile or a nod may be enough) or informative questions can be sufficient. Good human tutors know when to 'push' and when to 'back off'. They respond to non-verbal and to non-performance cues which can signify understanding, boredom and disappointment. They have an implicit awareness of the social context of learning, of the power that social support and social models can offer. In addition, they can call upon motivational strategies and the world knowledge they share with a student to illustrate and elucidate problem areas. Human tutors are aware of the social network in which learning takes place – the influence of peers, individual teachers and parents, together with the role an individual's own expectations and self-perceptions play in affecting the course of learning. The fields of cognitive, educational and social psychology are rich in their accounts of the many factors which can affect human performance. Human tutors are often aware of these because they are part of that social context, and they can call on this information to enhance the quality of their tutoring.

The term 'intelligent' is, in a sense misleading in the context of intelligent tutoring systems. Their current 'intelligence' lies in their ability to represent certain areas of human knowledge and expertise. Their potential 'intelligence' lies in the fact that they may be able to reflect a detailed model of the learner's state of understanding. From this, they may be able to identify preferred cognitive styles and may even offer remedial instruction in a range of teaching styles. Such would represent a major achievement, and would be of considerable assistance in the classroom. To achieve this, researchers and implementors need to know more about subject matters, more about learning, more about tutoring, more about individual differences in learning, and more about the interactions which exist between all these. Rosenberg (1987) throws a final dampener on the frequent high spirits and major claims of many ITS developers.

. . . ITS researchers might keep in mind the following conclusion . . . 'the potential benefits of CBI . . . all hinge upon the dedication, persistence, and ability of good teachers and courseware developers'. Of course, if there were enough dedicated, persistent, able teachers and course developers, and a social commitment to support them, would anyone be interested in ITSs?

10   *Misleading Visions?*

A Critical Consideration of the Role of Computers in Education

Jam tomorrow

Many texts on the use of computers in education offer a final chapter which presents a view of what might be on the horizon, given particular developments in computer-based technology. Frequently, the visions presented are based on software advances in artificial intelligence or in terms of hardware which will support a range of software developments. In general, the visions are optimistic, painting a picture of highly motivated pupils learning with the support of sophisticated electronic tools, which adapt to, and cater for, individual differences in ability, personality and aptitude. Such tools are often perceived as a panacea for what are seen as education's failings. Certainly, the visions which have been presented are seductively appealing, and there is little sign that educational computing is running short of visionaries. Perhaps the most recent feasible candidate for the 'jam tomorrow' scenario are the possibilities offered by the envisaged increased use of hypermedia within education, described by Jonassen (1988) as offering 'phenomenal potential' and being 'the most effective technology system to date for individualizing instruction'.

What is hypermedia?

Hypermedia can be seen as a development of 'hypertext' – a term used to describe the electronic representation of text which uses the random access capabilities of computers to break away from the sequential nature of print on paper. Hypermedia systems extend this non-linear representation to other forms of information transfer, including access to sound and moving and still images. The potential advantage for education is that vast amounts of information in a variety of media forms can be stored and accessed easily and rapidly via a variety of routes. Hypermedia environments can be structured in such a way that they enable high levels of user control. Thus, learners can access information following a set of guidelines or 'sign-posts', or they can, in effect, 'blaze new trails' according to individual preferences and inclinations.

Such systems usually involve more than a computer, and also incorporate linked mass storage devices such as interactive video or CD-ROM. Thus, for example, CD-ROMs (based on music compact-disc technology) have the potential to store more information than 700 double-sided floppy discs or the equivalent of 270,000 pages of text, 2000 high-resolution colour images, 200 hours of recorded speech, or any combination of these elements. However you look at it, this is a lot of information! So, it is possible to imagine a scenario in which a pupil seeking more information about life in the 1920s could have immediate access to copies of original newspaper items, fashions, personalities, music, politics, the possibilities determined by the availability of information in the database. The selection of one area of interest could lead to other aspects. Thus, a user opting for information on music could be offered a menu of choices, selection of one of which could provide extracts from original recordings. Further information could then be obtained on musicians, styles of music, its origins and its significance within a particular context. An imaginary scenario might involve selecting jazz as an option, which might lead to Louis Armstrong, leading to New Orleans, leading to the history and origins of jazz. Nor is such a scenario too far from reality. Apple computers gave 'The Apple Learning Disc', a sampler CD, to attendees of a conference on CD-ROM in Seattle in 1988. This disc, which operates on a CD drive linked to an Apple Macintosh, contains a range of options including information on American history, ancient Greek civilization and human anatomy. Selection of any one of the options results in an opening up of other possibilities. The American history option covers American life, politics and culture in the period 1800–1850, and consists of articles, images, maps, historical documents and sound recordings. Selection of any one of the options in American history leads to other information. Thus, selecting 'articles' provides the user with immediate access to a wide range of articles on American history during that period. In contrast, another selection will bring up visual and auditory information on the California Gold Rush.

The essence of such a system is that although all the information is stored, access to that information is determined by user choices of the options available. In this way, users explore the information following individual preferences, thereby, it is claimed, building on their own knowledge and understanding. Advocates of such hypermedia systems claim that they reflect current models of human associative memory and that they offer the potential to enhance thinking and learning because they structure information in a manner which is accessible to users' own knowledge structures (semantic networks). In an enthusiastic endorsement of hypermedia and CD-ROM Westby (1989) described the technology as '. . . the atomic bomb of the information age' which will '. . . break the barrier between learning and entertainment'.

Just a minute . . . haven't we been here before?

Some time has been spent on describing hypermedia and CD-ROM because it is a technology which is already available and which has potentially significant implications for education. In this sense, it offers an advantage in the visionary scenario, simply because the technology is a reality and not of the 'wait and see' variety. However, the enthusiasm being generated for such systems is strikingly reminiscent of earlier enthusiasms for computer applications in education, and it is perhaps worthwhile looking back in order to look forward.

The early to middle 1980s can be characterized as a period when there was great optimism concerning the potential use of computers in education. A brief overview of what some educational computer experts were saying reveals such optimism.

I believe that certain uses of very powerful computational technology and computational ideas can provide children with new possibilities for learning, thinking and growing emotionally as well as cognitively [pp. 17–18]. . . . my conjecture is that the computer can concretize (and personalize) the formal . . . . I believe that it can allow us to shift the boundary separating concrete and formal. [Papert, 1980, p. 21]

The computer may lead to new and entirely different modes of learning in our society, and these modes of learning may affect not only *how* we learn but, perhaps even more profoundly, *what* we learn. [Bork, 1985, p. 166]

The computer is a revolutionary tool that may have the potential to help children become more intelligent, effective individuals in a complex world. [Chaille and Littman, 1985]

Human–computer intelligence systems will serve to extend and ultimately to reorganize what we think of as human imagination, intelligence, problem-solving skills, and creativity. [Pea, 1985]

In my view the computer is an intellectual agent, operating in a culture and reflecting ideas of the culture . . . .. The computer becomes a medium for self-expression and for one's own intellectual development. [Solomon, 1986, p. 146]

A crucial part of learning is the development of self-awareness, the ability to reflect on what one is doing and thinking. In very particular ways, a teacher can use computer-based activities to facilitate this process. [Weir, 1987, p. 228]

A passing alien reflecting on such statements would probably conclude that use of computers in schools would have already had a major impact on the nature and content of children's learning. To what extent would such a conclusion have been valid?

Promises . . . promises

In general, the above draw attention to the potential role of the computer as a facilitator of higher-level cognition. This use of computers as a support tool in the development and exercise of high-level skills (problem solving, creativity, etc.) is probably most associated with Papert's advocacy of Logo (see Chapter 6). However, use of computers in this way is not restricted to Logo. The use of word processors (Chapter 8), desk-top publishing, ideas processors, databases, graphics packages and programming in languages other than Logo have all been proposed as potential supports for the development of general-purpose, *transferable* metacognitive skills. What links these various applications is a belief that in using the specific application, students will utilize a range of cognitive skills which will transfer and be applicable in a wide range of activities, both computer and non-computer based. Computers are perceived within such a framework as tools of the intellect (Olson, 1985).

Such a concept of the use of computers offers the potential of an expansion of human intellectual skills (Pea, 1985, also see discussion in Chapter 2). However, the question which must be asked is whether, at present, the research suggests that this is little more than a vision, and that the reality has yet to be attained. In general the evidence to date is not strongly supportive of the hypothesis that use of computers has resulted in clear evidence of the development of general cognitive skills. The literature on Logo, for example, consists of many anecdotal reports, of which the only consistency relates to high motivational appeal. Where controlled studies have been undertaken to attempt to quantify the effects of using Logo, the resultant findings have been variable. Thus, some authors have reported gains (e.g., Rieber, 1987; Horton and Ryva, 1986), whereas others have reported conflicting results (Pea, Kurland and Hawkins, 1985; Simon, 1987). Indeed, the very question of whether Logo is amenable to traditional methods of assessment has been questioned (Solomon, 1986). Other software has been claimed (by its producers) to encourage 'problem solving'. Dudley-Marling and Owston (1988) report some 350 software titles in this field. However, the effectiveness of few of these has been subject to experimental evaluation. Increasingly, Logo researchers have concentrated upon the nature and structure of Logo experiences and upon difficulties experienced when learning Logo (Fay and Mayer, 1987; Goodyear, 1987), rather than upon the question of whether using Logo leads to general cognitive gains. Such research concentrates upon the learners' mental models of the software or device being used, and is important as it has been argued that the user's mental model has a strong effect on subsequent performance (Hughes, Brackenridge and Macleod, 1987). If children are developing flawed models then it is possible that although they *may* acquire low level skills their inadequate models may prevent them from developing deeper conceptual understandings.

It might be argued that there is little need to subject such claims to rigorous evaluation, after all we do not evaluate the effectiveness of books in promoting reading skills. However, there is a broader issue at stake. Significant claims have been made concerning the potential of computers and certain types of software to result in the development of cognitive skills which are characteristic of high-level thinking. Such claims have a powerful appeal to teachers and to parents. As educators we have a responsibility to evaluate the validity of such claims. Research on the utlilization of higher-level skills like problem solving indicates that in order to utilize such skills it is necessary to have considerable specific knowledge about the area in question (domain-specific knowledge). Further, in order for transfer to occur, several conditions seem to be required: that learners possess the required domain-knowledge; that the situation to which transfer is expected is similar to one previously encountered, and that learners recognize that similarities exist. On the basis of such research about the development and transfer of general purpose skills, the isolated use of problem solving software seems unlikely to result in positive gains without considerable attention being paid to these other factors.

More criticisms!

The above represent a series of criticisms which reflect one trend in the literature related to the rationales often presented to justify the use of computers in education. However, they are by no means the only criticisms. As a delivery system, the styles of software commonly found can be seen as reflecting particular viewpoints of cognitive development and learning (see Chapters 3 and 4). In general, we can identify several distinct styles of software of relevance to education – drill and practice/tutorial, simulations, programming, utilities. These reflect a shift in the locus of control from tightly defined program control to increasing user freedom. Such a shift can be seen to mirror a shift in behaviourist-orientated approaches to learning (with links to Skinnerian views on learning) to more cognitive, child-centred perspectives (influenced by views originating with such theorists as Piaget and Bruner). In accepting such a dimension,

Striebel (1986) has argued that within a technological framework all these approaches reflect a shift towards technologizing education which 'delegitimize non-technological ways of learning and thinking about problems'. One of Striebel's major concerns is that an increasing use of computers in schools will come to reduce educational perspectives and aims which emphasize holistic approaches in which the child's entire development – intellectual, moral, social, emotional and physical – is nurtured. Similar reservations have been expressed by Scheffler (1986) and by Elkind (1985) who has pointed out that in our enthusiasm to promote and accelerate the development of intellectual skills in young children we might overlook the significance of childhood itself.

An underlying theme throughout this book has been that the application of computers in education brings both positive and negative aspects. Early criticisms of software presented to schools concentrated on the fact that they tended to be of a drill-and-practice nature, and thereby failed to incorporate current thinking on cognitive development. To a certain extent, the application of Logo can be seen as an attempt to move away from such software, to approaches which were more in accordance with dominant educational thinking. However, the use of Logo is not without its problems. Research has indicated that Logo has yet to fulfil its promise, and that the open-ended, discovery approach often associated with use of the language has been superseded by more structured approaches. In many ways, Logo encapsulates many of the problems which have emerged as experience in educational computing has evolved. Current issues centre on the nature of computer-mediated learning experiences; problems of design and evaluation of effective software; peer interactions; equity of access questions, and the recurrent problem of transfer of skills from computer-based experiences to non-computer situations.

Hypermedia

A cognitive solution?

Hypertext and hypermedia are currently being offered as one of the next major advances in computer-assisted learning. The development of such non-linear systems is perceived as offering the potential to deliver genuine individualization and interactivity – the 'Holy Grail' of educational computing. This promise is based in the fact that hypertext is not restricted to a linear form, but can be constructed with a multitude of available paths with a wide range of differing access points. Thus, learners can enter such knowledge systems with varying degrees of background knowledge and can follow or establish paths on the basis of their individual interests, expertise and information needs. A major reason why hypertext is seen as offering considerable potential for the development of more effective, individualized and interactive computer-mediated learning is that the flexibility and structure of such systems present the closest parallels to current thinking on human cognition.

Schema theory re-visited

According to schema theory, humans store information in knowledge structures known as schemata. A schema for an event, item or idea consists of attributes which are associations of individual forms around an idea on the basis of individual experience. Thus, my schema for football is constructed of information about the game of soccer, its rules, history, teams, competitions, events, personalities, etc. A schema for football held by a North American may refer to an entirely different game (American Football) with its own set of rules, history, events and idiosyncrasies. Our individual knowledge structures consist of schemata for these attributes. Thus, a schema for competition (within my football schema) will consist of information relating to competition, which can extend to different competitive sports, the nature of competition, the psychology of competition, etc. Within this, more schemata will be embedded, about sport, psychology, etc. What is within the individual schema and the links between schemata will be determined by personal experience. An individual's knowledge structure consists of schemata linked together by various associations within a semantic network. The structure of the semantic networks enables individuals to make sense of new information, store it and recall and infer from it on the basis of the associations within the networks.

Following on from this, it is but a short jump to regarding learning as consisting of constructing new associations and schemata and extending and modifying existing ones, i.e., the processes of assimilation and accommodation. It also follows within such a conceptualization of learning that if the material to be learnt/taught can be related to an individual's existing schemata the more easily such information will be acquired, stored and recalled. Any system which offers the potential to organize knowledge within a semantic network framework (i.e., links between concepts, ideas, etc.) and also provides the potential to enable individuals to relate that information to individual interests, knowledge, motivation, etc., offers a potentially powerful learning tool. Many believe that hypertext and hypermedia offer such possibilities.

A recipe for cognitive chaos?

The developments in hypertext and hypermedia appear to offer a practical way of realizing much of the claimed potential of computer-assisted learning, for example, individualization and interactivity. However, these promises are not without their problems.

As outlined earlier the development of hypermedia systems offers the opportunity for learners to create their own knowledge structures through multi-media access to vast amounts of information. Despite the appeal of this, problems are immediately apparent. Given the vast amounts of information available there is a tendency for learners to get lost in 'hyperspace' (Marchionini, 1988). Their chosen paths become disorientated, often because there are so many options available. Although user freedom offers many attractions, evidence suggests that many learners do not possess the higher-order skills necessary to make informed judgements concerning which options to pursue (Carrier, 1984). Distraction and potential confusion are compounded by the large amounts of easily accessible information and the exponentially greater number of learning options available to the learner. These increase the probability of cognitive overload, and the potential richness of the environment carries with it the risk that learners will lose their sense of goal direction with resultant confusion and loss of motivation. Within such a potentially open-ended environment, learners may choose to access information much of which may be only peripherally relevant to their main goals. An additional problem concerns the extent to which learners will be able to relate the information derived from hypertext explorations to their current knowledge, as the less structured the information, the more difficult it will be to carry out the processes of assimilation or accommodation. Access to and availability of information are not, in themselves, particularly satisfying educational goals. Of more significance are skills which enable learners to know where to find information, what questions to ask, and the significance of the information when they have found it. There is nothing inherent to hypertext or hypermedia systems which ensures that such skills will be utilized or developed. It is not knowledge that is power, but understanding.

Underlying these questions are fundamental issues of educational philosophy which address whether students should learn through browsing through the available information or by staying on task with clearly defined objectives. Educational and teaching philosophies will determine which scenario is preferable, but many current educational practices emphasize the importance of basic skill mastery and a product-orientated approach to learning, approaches which may be at odds with the open-ended, exploratory possibilities offered by hypermedia.

Re-inventing the wheel?

There is a very real sense in which educational computing seems to be on the verge of re-inventing the wheel. Many of the promises and problems surrounding the application of hypertext/hypermedia are those which have been raised in the context of other computer-mediated applications. They address issues of design, use, learner differences, educational philosophy and theories of learning. However, hypertext and hypermedia offer a major advantage over previous visions. This is that their flexibility and non-linearity offer the potential to structure information in a manner which accords to learners' own cognitive associative memory systems. To achieve this will require research on the design and use of hypertext. On the design side, questions which arise concern the degree of structure which should be incorporated; the semantic structure and links within the hypertext system (its knowledge structure) and how that can be related to the learner's knowledge structure; the extent to which guidance (sign-posts) should be provided; and how to facilitate the integration of hypertext information into user's cognitive structures. For potential users, there exist questions addressing the manner and depth of exploration; the activation of relevant knowledge, and the encoding of new information with existing information. These questions, of course, are not new. They relate to problems which have challenged educators for centuries, and some of them have even been raised in the context of computer-assisted learning! The past decade should have taught us to be wary of visionaries bearing computer-based gifts. The promises have been considerable, but research and experience suggest that those promises will only be realized as a result of considerable work on the part of teachers, researchers and developers. There is little reason to suppose that hypertext will be any different in the nature of the problems its use produces. However, where hypertext is unique within the history of educational technology is that 'its conceptual bases are implicitly cognitive' (Jonassen, 1988). Almost all authors in the field point out that the potential structure of hypertext matches that of human cognition, with its emphases on associations and relationships between ideas and concepts. To that extent, we should expect that

Hypertext will improve learning because it focuses attention on the relationships between ideas rather than isolated facts. (Kearsley, 1988)

Underlying this claim, however, is the assumption that this will be achieved only if the design of the hypertext systems is appropriate for its potential users.

Conclusion

This book started with a psychological perspective, and ends with one. Current developments appear to offer the potential of computer-based cognitive tools which parallel human memory systems. As such, we should expect cognitive scientists to be deeply involved in the design of hypertext learning materials.

Jonassen (1988) has pointed out that 'Cognitive psychology provides rich conceptualizations to guide its production' and that 'hypertext offers a powerful environment for conducting studies in cognitive psychology'. He also points out that this potential is, as yet, relatively unexplored and that relatively little research has been carried out to investigate the cognitive effects of interacting with hypertext systems. The term 'hype' is frequently associated with the use of exaggerated or intensive publicity. It is a term which can be applied to some of the earlier claims for the educational uses of computers. The publicity associated with hypertext and hypermedia is in a similar vein. The hope is that it will not come to have the same connotations for hypertext, and that this time we can really deliver on our promises.

References

Ault, R. L. (1977) *Children's Cognitive Development: Piaget's theory and the process approach*, New York: Oxford University Press.

Bandura, A. (1977) 'Self-efficacy: toward a unifying theory of behavioral change', *Psychological Review*, 84, 191–215.

Bartlett, F. C. (1932) *Remembering: A study in experimental and social psychology*, London: Cambridge University Press.

Bell, M. E. (1985) 'The role of instructional theories in the evaluation of microcomputer courseware', *Educational Technology*, March, 36–40.

Bereiter, C. and Scardamelia, M. (1983) 'Schooling and the growth of intentional cognition: helping children take charge of their own minds', in Lamm, Z., (ed.) *New Trends in Education*, Tel Aviv: Yachdev United Publishing Company.

Bork, A. (1985) *Personal Computers in Education*, NewYork: Harper and Row.

Bortner, M. and Birch, H. G. (1962) 'Perceptual and perceptual motor dissociation in cerebral palsied children', *Journal of Nervous and Mental Diseases*, 134(2), 103–8.

Bortner, M. and Birch, H. G. (1970) 'Cognitive capacity and cognitive performance', *American Journal of Mental Deficiency*, 74, 735–44.

Bower, T. G. R. (1979) *Development in Infancy*, San Francisco: Freeman.

Brock, P. A. (1988) 'The logicreative approach: how to teach Logo successfully', in Collins, J. H., N. Estes and D. Walker (eds), *Proceedings of the Fifth International Conference on Technology and Education*, Edinburgh: CEP Consultants.

Brown, J. S. (1985) 'Process *versus* product: a perspective on tools for communal and informal electronic learning', in Chen, M. and W. Paisley (eds) *Children and Microcomputers: Research on the newest medium*, Beverly Hills: Sage.

Brown, J. S. and Burton, R. R. (1978) 'Diagnostic models for procedural bugs in basic mathematical skills', *Cognitive Science*, 2, 155–92.

Brownell, W. A. (1928) *The Development of Children's Number Ideas*, Chicago: The University of Chicago.

Bruner, J. S. (1966) *Toward a Theory of Instruction*, New York: Norton.

Bruner, J. S. (1983) *Child's Talk: Learning to use language*, Oxford: Oxford University Press.

Burton, R. R. and Brown, J. S. (1979) 'An investigation of computer coaching for informal learning activities', *International Journal of Man–Machine Studies*, 11, 5–24.

Carrier, C. (1984) 'Do learners make good choices?', *Instructional Innovator*, February, 15–17.

Chaille, C. and Littman, B. (1985) 'Computers in early education: the child as theory builder', in Klein, E. L. (ed.) *Children and Computers: New directions for child development, No. 28*, San Francisco: Jossey Bass.

Chandler, D. (1984) *Young Learners and the Microcomputer*, Milton Keynes: Open University Press.

Clancy, W. J. (1984) 'Methodology for building an intelligent tutoring system', in Kintsch, W. (ed.) *Methods and Tactics in Cognitive Science*, Hillsdale: Erlbaum.

Clarke, A. D. B. and Hermelin, H. F. (1955) 'Adult imbeciles: their abilities and trainability', *The Lancet*, ii, 337–9.

Clements, D. H. (1986) 'Effects of Logo and CAI environments on cognition and creativity', *Journal of Educational Psychology*, 78(4), 309–18.

Clements, D. H. and Gullo, D. F. (1984) 'Effects of computer programming on young children's cognition', *Journal of Educational Psychology*, 76(6), 1051–8.

Cohen, R. and Geva, E. (1986) 'Introducing Logo to young children: a developmental approach', paper presented at Annual meeting of the Canadian Society for the Study of Children , Winnipeg, June 1986.

Cronbach, L. J. and Snow, R. E. (1977) *Aptitudes and Instructional Methods: A handbook for research on interactions*, New York: Irvington.

Cumming, G. (1988) 'Artificial intelligence applications to learning and training', Economic and Social Research Council (UK) *Information Technology in Education Research Programme*, occasional paper, InTER/2/88.

Daiute, C. (1985) *Writing and Computers*, Reading (Mass.): Addison-Wesley.

de Charms, R. (1968) *Personal Causation*, New York: Academic Press.

de Charms, R. (1976) *Enhancing Motivation Change in the Classroom*, New York: Irvington.

Deci, E. L. (1975) *Intrinsic Motivation*, New York: Plenum.

Dewey, J. (1933) *How We Think*, New York: Heath.

Doise, W. and Mugny, G. (1984) *The Social Development of Intellect*, Oxford: Pergamon.

Donaldson, M. (1978) *Children's Minds*, London: Fontana.

du Boulay, B. and Sloman, A. (1988) 'Bread today, jam tomorrow: the impact of AI on education', in Collins, J. H., N. Estes and D. Walker (eds), *Proceedings of the Fifth International Conference on Technology and Education*, Edinburgh: CEP Consultants.

Dudley-Marling, C. and Owston, R. D. (1988) 'Using microcomputers to teach problem solving', *Educational Technology*, July, 27–33.

Eisenstein, E. L. (1979) *The Printing Press as an Agent of Change*, New York: Cambridge University Press.

Elkind, D. (1985) 'The impact of computer use on cognitive development in young children: a theoretical analysis, *Computers in Human Behavior*, 1, 131–41.

Ellis, A. B. (1974) *The Use and Misuse of Computers in Education*, New York: McGraw-Hill.

Fay, A. L. and Mayer, R. E. (1987) 'Children's naive conceptions and confusions about Logo graphics commands', *Journal of Educational Psychology*, 79(3), 254–68.

Feigenbaum, E. A. and McCorduck, P. (1984) *The Fifth Generation: Artificial intelligence and Japan's computer challenge to the world*, London: Michael Joseph.

Gagne, R. M. (1970) *The Conditions of Learning*, London: Holt, Rinehart and Winston.

Gagne, R. M. (1975) *Essentials of Learning for Instruction*, Hinsdale: Dryden.

Gagne, R. M. (1982) 'Developments in learning psychology: implications for instructional design; and effects of computer technology on instructional design and development' (an interview with R. M. Gagne) *Educational Technology*, June, 11–15.

Gagne, R. M. and Briggs, L. J. (1979) *Principles of Instructional Design*, New York: Holt, Rinehart and Winston.

Geoffrion, L. D. and Goldenberg, E. P. (1981) 'Computer-based exploratory learning systems for communication-handicapped children', *Journal of Special Education*, 15, 325–32.

Goldenberg, E. P. (1979) *Special Technology for Special Children*, Baltimore: University Park Press.

Goldenberg, E. P., Russell, S. J. and Carter, C. J. (1984) *Computers, Education and Special Needs*, Reading (Mass.): Addison-Wesley.

Goodyear, P. (1987) 'Sources of difficulty in assessing the cognitive effects of learning to program', *Journal of Computer Assisted Learning*, 3, 214–23.

Graves, D. H. (1979) 'Research update: what children show us about revision', *Language Arts*, 56(3), 312–19.

Graves, D. H. (1983) *Writing: Teachers and children at work*, Exeter (UK): Heinemann.

Greenfield, P. M. (1984) *Mind and Media: The effects of television, computers and video games*, Aylesbury (UK): Fontana.

Halliday, M. A. K. (1975) *Learning How To Mean: Explorations in the development of language*, London: Edward Arnold.

Hartley, J. R. and Sleeman, D. H. (1973) 'Towards more intelligent teaching systems', *International Journal of Man–Machine Studies*, 2, 215–36.

Havelock, E. A. (1973) 'Prologue to Greek literacy', in Boulter, C. (ed.) *Lectures in Memory of Louise Taft Semple*, second series, 1966–71, Cincinnati: University of Oklahoma Press for the University of Cincinnati.

Hawkridge, D., Vincent, T. and Hales, D. (1985) *New Information Technology in the Education of Disabled Children and Adults*, London: Croom Helm.

Horton, J. and Ryva, K. (1986) 'Assessing learning with Logo: A pilot study', *The Computing Teacher*, August/September, 24–8.

Hughes, M. (1975) 'Egocentrism in pre-school children', unpublished Doctoral dissertation, University of Edinburgh.

Hughes, M., Brackenridge, A. and Macleod, H. (1987) 'Children's ideas about computers', in Rutkowska, J. C. and C. Crook (eds) *Computers, Cognition and Development: Issues for psychology and education*, Chichester: Wiley.

Jonassen, D. (1988) 'Designing structured hypertext and structuring access to hypertext', *Educational Technology*, November, 13–16.

Kearsley, G. (1988) 'Authoring considerations for hypertext', *Educational Technology*, November, 21–4.

Keller, J. M. (1983) 'Motivational design of instruction', in Reigeluth, C. M (ed.) *Instructional-Design Theories and Models: An overview of their current status*, Hillsdale: Erlbaum.

Kephart, N. C. (1971) *The Slow Learner in the Classroom*, Columbus: Merrill.

Killian, E. W. (1967) 'New approaches to teach children, hitherto crucial crib cases', unpublished paper presented at the 91st Meeting of the American Association of Mental Deficiency.

Krashen, S. D. (1984) *Writing: Research, theory and applications*, Oxford: Pergamon Institute of English.

Landa, L. N. (1974) *Algorithmisation in Learning and Instruction*, Englewood Cliffs, NJ: Educational Technology Publications.

Landa, L. N. (1982) 'The improvement of instruction, learning and perform-ance: potential of 'Landamatic Theory' for teachers, instructional designers and materials producers', an interview with L. N. Landa, *Educational Technology*, Part I, October, 7–12; Part II, November, 7–14.

Landesman-Dwyer, S. (1974) 'A description and modification of the behavior of nonambulatory profoundly mentally retarded children', unpublished Doctoral dissertation: University of Washington.

Lawler, R. W. (1982) 'Designing computer microworlds', *Byte*, 7, 138–60.

Lawler, R. W. (1985) *Computer Experience and Cognitive Development: A Child's Learning in a Computer Culture*, Chichester: Ellis Horwood.

Lepper, M. R. (1985) 'Microcomputers in education: motivational and social issues', *American Psychologist*, 40(1), 1–18.

Leron, U. (1985) 'Logo today: vision and reality', *The Computing Teacher*, February, 26–32.

Lumsdaine, A. A. (1964) 'Educational technology: issues and problems', in Lange, P. C. (ed.) *Programmed Instruction: The Sixty-Sixth Yearbook of the National Society for the Study of Education*, Chicago: NSSE.

Malone, T. W. (1981) 'Toward a theory of intrinsically motivating instruction', *Cognitive Science*, 4, 333–69.

Malone, T. W. and Lepper, M. R. (1983) 'Making learning fun: a taxonomy of intrinsic motivation for learning', in Snow, R. E. and M. L. Farr (eds) *Aptitude, Learning and Instruction: III conative and affective process analyses*, Hillsdale: Erlbaum.

Marchionini, G. (1988) 'Hypermedia and learning: freedom and chaos', *Educational Technology*, November, 8–12.

Mayer, R. E. (1981) *The Promise of Cognitive Psychology*, San Francisco: Freeman.

Mayer, R. E. (1983) *Thinking, Problem Solving, Cognition*, San Francisco: Freeman.

Mills, G. M. (1985) 'Categories of educational microcomputer programs: theories of learning and implications for future research', in Alloway, G. S. and G. M. Mills (eds) *New Directions in Education and Training Technology*, London: Kogan Page.

Murphy, R. J. and Doughty, N. R. (1977) 'Establishment of controlled arm movements in profoundly retarded students using response contingent vibratory simulation', *American Journal of Mental Deficiency*, 82(2), 212–16.

Neisser, U. (1967) *Cognition and Reality: Principles and implications of cognitive psychology*, San Francisco: Freeman.

Nichol, J. (1988) 'Roles for microworlds', in Lewis, R. (ed.) *Learning Through Microworlds*, Economic and Social Research Council (UK) Occasional Paper ITE/26/88.

Nickerson, R. (1983) 'Computer programming as a vehicle for teaching thinking skills', *Thinking: The Journal of Philosophy for Children*, 4, 42–8.

Nicolson, R. J. (1988) 'The SUMIT intelligent arithmetic tutor', in Collins, J. H., N. Estes and D. Walker (eds) *Proceedings of the Fifth International Conference on Technology and Education*, Edinburgh: CEP Consultants.

Norman, D. A. (1982) *Learning and Memory*, San Francisco: Freeman.

Norman, D. A. and Rumelhart, D. E. (1975) *Explorations in Cognition*, San Francisco: Freeman.

Odor, J. P. (1988) 'Computer toolkits in special education', in Collins, J. H., N. Estes and D. Walker (eds) *Proceedings of the Fifth International Conference on Technology and Education*, Edinburgh: CEP Consultants.

Olson, D. R. (1976) 'Culture, technology and intellect', in Resnick, L. B. (ed.) *The Nature of Intelligence*, Hillsdale: Erlbaum.

Olson, D. R. (1985) 'Computers as tools of the intellect', *Educational Researcher*, 14(5), 5–8.

O'Shea, T. and Self, J. (1983) *Learning and Teaching With Computers: Artificial intelligence in education*, Brighton: Harvester.

Papert, S. (1980) *Mindstorms: Children, computers and powerful ideas*, Brighton: Harvester.

Pea, R. D. (1985) 'Integrating human and computer intelligence', in Klein, E. L. (ed.) *Children and Computers: New directions for child development, No. 28*, San Francisco: Jossey Bass.

Pea, R. D., Kurland, D. M. and Hawkins, J. (1985) 'Logo and the development of thinking skills', in Chen, M. and W. Paisley (eds) *Children and Microcomputers: Research on the newest medium*, Beverly Hills: Sage.

Peacock, M. (1988) 'Handwriting *versus* wordprocessed print: an investigation into teachers' grading of English language and literature essay work at 16+', *Journal of Computer Assisted Learning*, 4(3), 162–72.

Piaget, J. (1971) *Science of Education and the Psychology of the Child*, New York: Viking.

Pulaski, M. A. B. (1971) *Understanding Piaget*, New York: Harper and Row.

Reiber, L. P. (1987) 'LOGO and its promise: a research report', *Educational Technology*, February, 12–16.

Reigeluth, C. M. (1983) *Instructional-Design Theories and Models: An overview of their current status*, Hillsdale: Erlbaum.

Robinson, J. (1980) 'Psychiatry and Marxism', *Labour Review*, 4(1).

Rosenberg, R. (1987) 'A critical analysis of research on intelligent tutoring systems', *Educational Technology*, November 1988.

Ross, P. (1987) 'Intelligent tutoring systems', *Journal of Computer Assisted Instruction*, 3, 194–203.

Rostron, A. B. and Lovett, S. (1981) 'A new outlook with the computer', *Special Education: Forward trends*, 8(4), 29–31.

Rubincam, I. (1987) 'Frequently cited authors in the literature on computer applications to education', *Journal of Computer-Based Instruction*, 14(4), 150–6.

Rubincam, I. and Olivier, W. P. (1985) 'An investigation of limited learner-control options in a CAI mathematics course', *AEDS Journal*, Summer, 211–26.

Rushby, N. J. (1979) *An Introduction to Educational Computing*, London: Croom Helm.

Sage, M. W. and Smith, D. J. (1983) *Microcomputers in Education: A framework for research*, London: Social Science Research Council.

Schank, R. (1982) *Dynamic Memory*, Cambridge: Cambridge University Press.

Scheffler, I. (1986) 'Computers at school?', *Teachers College Record*, 87(4), 513–28.

Scribner, S. (1969) 'The cognitive consequences of literacy', unpublished paper, City University of New York.

Self, J. (1985) 'A perspective on intelligent computer-assisted learning', *Journal of Computer Assisted Learning*, 1, 159–66.

Seligman, M. E. (1975) *Helplessness*, San Francisco: Freeman.

Sewell, D. F. and Rotheray, D. R. (1987) 'Our children can't do that! The under-estimation of ability: implications for software design', *European Journal of Special Needs Education*, 2(2), 103–10.

Sharples, M. (1985) 'Phrasebooks and boxes: microworlds for language', in Duncan, K. and D. Harris (eds) *Proceedings of the World Conference in Education*, North Holland: Elsevier Science Publications.

Simon, T. (1987) 'Claims for Logo: who should we believe and why?', in Rutkowska, J. C. and C. Crook (eds) *Computers, Cognition and Development: Issues for psychology and education*, Chichester: Wiley.

Skillen, P. (1986) 'Transfers on the train of thoughts', paper presented to the Educational Computing Organisation of Ontario, Logo Special Interest Group.

Sleeman, D. (1987) 'Cognitive science, AI and developmental psychology. Are there links? Could there be links?', in Rutkowska, J. C. and C. Crook (eds) *Computers, Cognition and Development: Issues for psychology and education*, Chichester: Wiley.

Sloman, A. (1978) *The Computer Revolution in Philosophy*, Brighton: Harvester.

Solomon, C. (1986) *Computer Environments for Children: A reflection on theories of learning and education*, Cambridge (Mass.): MIT Press.

Striebel, M. J. (1986) 'A critical analysis of the use of computers in education', *Educational Communication and Technology Journal*, 34(5), 137–61.

Suppes, P. and Morningstar, M. (1969) 'Computer-assisted instruction', *Science*, 166, 343–50.

Thorndike, E. L. (1913) *Educational Psychology: Vol. II The psychology of learning*, New York: Teachers College, Columbia University.

Thorndike, E. L. (1922) *The Psychology of Arithmetic*, New York: The Macmillan Company.

Turkle, S. (1984) *The Second Self: Computers and the human spirit*, New York: Simon and Schuster.

UNESCO (1986) *Informatics and Education: A first survey of the state of the art in 43 countries*, Paris: UNESCO.

UNESCO (1989) *Education and Informatics: Strengthening international co-operation*, Paris: UNESCO.

Vygotsky, L. S. (1978) *Mind in Society: The development of higher psychological processes*, Cambridge (Mass.): Harvard University Press.

Walker, D. F. (1983) 'Reflections on the educational potential and limitations of computers', *Phi Delta Kappan*, October, 103–7.

Ward, R. D. (1989) 'Some uses of natural language interfaces in computer-assisted language learning', *Instructional Science*, 18, 45–61.

Weiner, B. (1978) *Human Motivation*, New York: Holt, Rinehart and Winston.

Weir, S. (1981) 'Logo and the exceptional child', *Microcomputing*, September, 76–83.

Weir, S. (1987) *Cultivating Minds: A Logo casebook*, New York: Harper and Row.

Weizenbaum, J. (1976) *Computer Power and Human Reason*, Harmondsworth (UK): Penguin.

Westby, M. (1989) 'Inventing the future', *MacUser*, October, 39–43.

Zajonc, A. G. (1984) 'Computer pedagogy? Questions concerning the new educational technology', *Teachers College Record*, 85(4), 569–77.

Zeitschel, K. A., Kalish, R. A. and Colarrusso, R. (1979) 'Visual perception tests used with physically handicapped children', *Academic Therapies*, 14, 565–76.

Author Index

Subject Index